Personal Counseling Office
Penn State Erie, The Behrend College
5091 Station Road
Erie, PA 16563

-THE-
Rape Recovery
HANDBOOK

Step-by-Step

Help for

Survivors of

Sexual Assault

APHRODITE MATSAKIS, PH.D.

New Harbinger Publications, Inc.

Publisher's Note

This publication is designed to provide accurate and authoritative information in regard to the subject matter covered. It is sold with the understanding that the publisher is not engaged in rendering psychological, financial, legal, or other professional services. If expert assistance or counseling is needed, the services of a competent professional should be sought.

Distributed in Canada by Raincoast Books

Copyright © 2003 by Aphrodite Matsakis
New Harbinger Publications, Inc.
5674 Shattuck Avenue
Oakland, CA 94609

Cover design by Amy Shoup
Edited by Kayla Sussell
Text design by Tracy Marie Carlson

ISBN 1-57224-337-6 Paperback

New Harbinger Publications' Web site address: www.newharbinger.com

05   04   03

10   9   8   7   6   5   4   3   2   1

First printing

This book is dedicated to all who have suffered as the result of a sexual assault. It is also dedicated to the many individuals who have worked tirelessly, often with little or no compensation, to promote public awareness of sexual assault, to increase and provide services for sexual assault survivors, and to institute needed legal reforms.

I would also like to dedicate my work to all those who have offered, and continue to offer, compassion and assistance to sexual assault survivors in their struggle to reclaim their sense of personal power and their faith in life.

Contents

Acknowledgments

I would like to thank the staff of New Harbinger Publications for their support and assistance, especially Kayla Sussell whose careful and creative editing of this book contributed greatly to its organization and clarity. I would also like to thank the social science researchers, sexual assault counselors, and other mental health professionals whose knowledge of sexual assault helped make this book possible. Most of all, I would like to acknowledge the many victims of sexual assault who survived to tell their stories and had the courage to share with others some of the most horrible moments of their lives.

I owe a special debt of gratitude to those sexual assault survivors who have trusted me enough to share their pain with me. They have served as models of inspiration in their efforts to bear what, for most people, would be unbearable emotional pain. That pain is often accompanied by physical pain and undeserved social rejection, as well. Despite their many hardships, most of the sexual assault survivors whose stories were contributed to this book have striven and have succeeded in making a positive difference in the lives of others.

Introduction

My personality is like a house with many rooms. Being sexually assaulted was like lightning striking my house. The fire destroyed my bedroom and some of the adjoining rooms, and the rooms that escaped the fire smelled like smoke. So I couldn't be anywhere in the house without remembering the assault. The rooms that had reflected my sense of security, sexuality, and self-confidence were utterly gone, as were my hopes for the future. The rooms left standing were like my relationships, damaged but not completely ruined. My cats survived and my computer was intact, but all I could focus on was the smell of stale smoke.

Determined not to let the rapist ruin my life, I forced myself to get back to "normal" as soon as possible. Everyone was amazed at how quickly I recovered. But I had started drinking, and overeating, too; not knowing why, knowing only that I had to, lest something terrible should happen. But the terrible thing had already happened—I had been assaulted.

When I started missing workdays because I could not get out of bed, I realized my pretence of recovery was over. As hard as it was—and it was hard—I went to see a counselor. With her help, I learned to view my assault in a new light, and I found ways to get through my dark days without alcohol or extra food. I also joined a survivors group. The emotional and spiritual intimacy of the group helped to strengthen me.

My house is being rebuilt now. Despite the new furniture, the burnt ruins are a permanent part of my brain. Whenever sexual assault is on the news, I find myself back in those rooms, sad, angry, and scared. But I'm not locked in those rooms anymore. I have some keys now—coping skills. If I just use them, I can escape and not allow the memories to trap me.

My coping skills are good fire extinguishers, too. I need them when the memories of the rapist's touch make me feel as though I'm being burned alive at the stake, or when my anger feels like a wildfire that wants to destroy everything in sight. My fire extinguishers don't put out the fire entirely, but they sure help.

Yesterday was the first day my house didn't smell of smoke. As I passed by the rooms that had been rebuilt, I didn't even think of the ruined ones they had replaced. I never thought that day would happen. Maybe I'm finally beginning to heal and maybe, someday, the assault will no longer be the defining moment of my life.

—Patricia, sexual assault survivor

Patricia's first step toward healing from sexual assault was to take the risk of reaching out for help. Congratulations! You've just done the same. You not only bought this book (or borrowed it), but you have begun to read it!

Many women describe sexual assault as the worst experience of their lives. Indeed, except for homicide, sexual assault is the most serious violation of a person's physical, emotional, and spiritual self that anyone can experience. It takes tremendous inner strength and great self-love to recover from the cruelty of sexual assault.

The myth that sexual assault means being attacked at night in a dark alley by a stranger with a weapon is deeply imbedded in our national psyche. "It can't be rape unless he has a weapon or unless she is battered," is a common misconception. Because of such ideas, women who are assaulted without the use of a weapon or physical force, or women who are attacked by a date, partner, family member, or a trusted professional sometimes wonder if they were "really" sexually assaulted.

Do you, like many others, ask yourself one of these common questions: "Is it rape if he didn't have a gun or a knife? Is it rape if he used emotional pressure to coerce you into sexual activities?

Is it rape if there was anal or oral sex, such as fellatio or cunnilingus, instead of intercourse? Is it rape if he put his finger, a stick, or a banana inside of you instead of his penis? Is it rape if he ejaculated outside, rather than inside, of you? Is it rape if he didn't ejaculate, lost his erection before he entered you, or entered only partway or only for a few seconds?

The answer to all of these questions is a resounding "yes!" Being forced to masturbate or to masturbate someone else, and being subjected to unnecessary internal examinations by a doctor or nurse are also forms of sexual assault.

In this book, sexual assault is defined as *any form of nonconsensual sexual contact.* Sexual contact refers to another person touching any of the sexual parts of your body (the inner thighs, breasts, buttocks, genitals, or anus) with a part of their body or an object. Nonconsensual sexual contact includes that which takes place when a woman is unconscious or incapable of true consent due to mental defect, mental or physical illness, or is incapacitated as the result of alcohol or drug intake or undergoing a medical procedure. Consent is also not possible in situations of unequal power, such as when a male is older, physically stronger, or more emotionally mature than a woman or if he holds some form of economic or social power over her.

The specific legal definitions of rape, sexual battery, sexual misconduct, and other forms of sexual assault vary from state to state. Yet all states consider rape, which involves penetration, however slight, as the most serious form of sexual assault. Nevertheless, all forms of sexual assault are an outrage. Regardless of what others think, if in your heart you feel you were sexually assaulted and that the assault has damaged your life, this book can help you to heal.

Sexual Assault's Physical and Psychological Aftermath

During the assault, most victims feel terrified, helpless, humiliated, and confused. In some instances, however, the fear is so great that it is suppressed. Both fighting back and its opposite, going numb, are common. Afterward, any of these feelings can persist, especially the terror. Even when an offender is incarcerated or dead, his victim can fear that he, or another assailant, might be around any corner, ready to attack again.

Once a victim becomes angry, she can direct fury not only toward the offender, but toward anyone whom she feels degraded her or ignored her pain, including police and legal officials, helping professionals, and her loved ones. Even if she is supported by others and victorious in the legal system, she may become furious because of her disappointment that neither others' support nor success in court was enough to end her inner turmoil.

Often, her terror and rage alternate with periods of numbing. Such cycling—between being constantly alert for danger and feeling emotionally shutdown—may create emotional instability which undermines the victim's self-confidence and, often, her relationships and ability to function.

Many survivors develop post-traumatic stress disorder (PTSD) or depression and physical problems, such as nausea; fatigue; genital-urinary, skin, sleep, and appetite problems; head-, stomach-, and backaches; and pelvic and other physical pains. Prior medical or psychiatric problems tend to worsen, and social and work relationships tend to suffer.

When a victim seeks relief in alcohol or another addiction, her problems mount and her self-esteem plummets even farther. Her faith in the world, other people, and herself almost broken, the victim can easily decide she is a failure and fall into despair. As stated by one survivor, "Think of the lowest thing in the world, and whatever it is, I'm lower" (Forward and Buck 1978, 91).

Sexual assault turns you into both a victim and a survivor. You were victimized once when you were rendered helpless in a situation of great danger. Then, if you received any rejecting, callous, or impersonal treatment from others, you were victimized again. The term "victim" recognizes the cruelty and unfairness of sexual assault and puts the responsibility for the assault where it belongs—on the assailant. Yet it is even more important to recognize your determination to make the most of your life. In this book you will be referred to as a *survivor* more often than as a victim to emphasize a truth more significant than victimization: the human capacity to bear what seems unbearable and to keep on growing, in spite of the wreckage of the past.

Cautions

You must proceed on the healing journey at your own pace. You must also carefully monitor yourself so that you do not become so distressed that the rest of your life is seriously impaired. It is for these reasons that certain cautions must be observed.

While you are working with this book, if you experience any of the following reactions, seek professional help immediately and do not continue reading this text without first consulting your physician or a licensed mental health counselor: memory problems; feeling disoriented or out of touch with reality, even temporarily; hallucinations; extremely vivid flashbacks; suicidal or homicidal thoughts; self-destructive behavior, such as substance abuse or self-mutilation; hyperventilation; uncontrollable shaking; irregular heartbeat; extreme nausea; diarrhea; hemorrhaging; increased symptoms of a preexisting medical or psychiatric problem; or any intense, new, or unexplained pains.

You can expect to feel quite sad, anxious, numb, or angry as you work with this book, but this does not mean that you are mentally or morally deficient or that you will never recover. Most likely your intense reactions reflect the severity of the assault or of other stresses in your life.

At times, your emotions may be so strong, they feel overwhelming. You need not become alarmed at feeling overwhelmed if it subsides within a short time and you regain enough emotional and mental balance so that you can function. On the other hand, if it takes a long time for your emotional pain and mental confusion to subside, or if they do not subside enough so that you can resume functioning, you must contact a mental health professional immediately or to go the emergency room of a local hospital.

This Book's Goals

This book hopes to restore your self-esteem and to reduce, if not eliminate, any feelings of guilt, shame, or humiliation you may be feeling as the result of the assault by helping you to acquire a more rational view of your sexual assault. Because of the close relationship between your thoughts and feelings, the more realistically and logically you can learn to think about the assault, the more you can expect your suffering to diminish.

The focus of the book is on a cognitive or intellectual analysis of your sexual assault. Although some guidance will be given for managing anxiety, anger, and numbing, this book does not offer a complete trauma-processing program. You will need to supplement the suggestions you will find here with those in more specialized self-help books or in treatment with a trained mental health professional. (See appendixes A and B: Getting Help, and Resources.)

It is also beyond this book's scope to offer guidance for confronting an abusive family member or another assailant. Furthermore, this book is not for persons suffering from multiple personality disorder or schizophrenia. If you are struggling with a financial, family, medical, or other personal crisis or with a severe medical or psychiatric problem, your priority must be coping with the present, not exploring the past.

If you are currently being physically or sexually abused, you need professional, legal, and other types of assistance immediately. Consult appendix B for guidance.

If you have been sexually assaulted more than once, especially if you were a child at the time of the assaults, working with this book may be extremely difficult. Work on one assault at a time. Then, if you choose to, repeat the process for another attack.

At times, recovery may seem impossible. However, like many other survivors of childhood abuse, you can go on to find meaning, joy, and love in your life, despite your horrendous past. Because of the enormity of your pain, you may have to work harder and longer for it. Professional help may also be needed.

How This Book Can Help You

The more you know about sexual assault, the better you will understand what happened to you and be able to put it into perspective. This book describes the nature of sexual assault and the ways it can affect your emotional and physical health. Appendixes A and B will direct you to hot lines, organizations, books, and other sources of information and help.

Knowledge is necessary, but it is not enough. The assault shattered your faith in others and yourself, perhaps convincing you that you are incompetent and worthless and doomed to a life of misery. The first and most important step in recovery is to restore your faith in yourself. Once you can make a clear connection between the assault and your sense of worthlessness and hopelessness, the negative impact of the assault can begin to lose its power over your life.

Here, in a step-by-step fashion, you will examine your negative reactions in light of the realities of sexual assault and of certain illogical thinking patterns, such as thinking that you can predict the future or act perfectly under extreme stress. You will learn how to dispute these and other irrational ideas, such as the notion that you are now, and forever will be, "damaged goods," undesirable to everyone and undeserving of anyone's respect.

Your attacker overpowered you once; don't let him usurp the rest of your life. Your commitment to recovery is a way of fighting back—it is the healthiest kind of revenge. It will be a struggle, but it is possible to succeed.

How to Use This Book

Read slowly and work on the written exercises at your own pace so that you do not become overly anxious, angry, or numb. You may sense intuitively when you need to stop to process what you have read or written. You may also need to stop to soothe yourself. After finishing a chapter and doing the exercises, congratulate yourself for what you have accomplished. Or, if you needed to stop to soothe yourself, applaud yourself for listening to yourself compassionately rather than forcing yourself to continue.

To help you monitor your reactions, at the end of each chapter you will be asked to check in with yourself, that is, to determine how you feel after finishing the chapter and doing the exercises.

How This Book Is Organized

This book has three parts. Chapters 1 through 4 prepare you for the recovery process by helping you to set healthy limits on your efforts, tend to your physical health and safety, build a support system, and learn to manage troubling states, such as anxiety. Chapters 5 through 7 provide factual information about sexual assault and its emotional and physical repercussions. In chapters 8 through 11 you will examine your reactions to the assault in light of a number of irrational mindsets, then you will learn how to dispel the irrational ideas about the assault which may be the source of much unnecessary shame, guilt, and self-loathing.

Questionnaires and Exercises: Keeping a Journal

Simply reading this book will not produce significant change. If you expect to have any long-term recovery from sexual assault, you must complete the writing assignments. Writing about painful experiences, especially in longhand, can help you to see them more clearly and to release them.

Writing in longhand is recommended over typing because of the tendency to write more extensively and in more depth about negative experiences and emotions in longhand. It is more personal than typing because there is less physical space between you and your writing. Also, the more official-looking nature of typed script, as compared to your unique handwriting, might inhibit you from expressing your angers, insecurities, and other uncomfortable emotions. The release of the negativity is especially healing. It also has been found that writing about the specific events of a trauma and the feelings involved can boost the immune system for at least six weeks after the writing of such a description (Esterling et al. 1999).

Working through this book is a process. This means that you will reread, reevaluate, and expand on your work as you go along. For that reason, you need to keep a journal that consists of all the writing you do to complete the exercises. Even if you already keep a personal diary, you need to have a separate "sexual assault healing" journal to work with this book for maximum benefit.

Feel free to change any specifics in the exercises to fit your experience. For example, if a question refers to your attacker as a male and your attacker was a female, substitute "she" for "he" and so forth. The more honest and thorough you are in completing these exercises, the more deeply you can heal.

I recommend buying a three-ring binder, some dividers, and some loose-leaf paper. Because you will be asked to go back, reread, and add to the writing you have already done for previous exercises, using a loose- leaf notebook will enable you to add sheets as necessary. You will also be asked to write on a number of specific topics, such as shame. The dividers will make each topic easy to find when you need it. You may decorate the binder if you wish to, or you can leave it plain and undecorated.

It will be fine to skip around while reading, but the exercises follow a logical order. Some of the exercises will be impossible to complete without having completed previous writing assignments. However, if a particular section or exercise seems too distressing for you, skip it.

You will write this journal for yourself, not for an English class. Try not to judge what you are writing. Let it flow out of your heart, mind, and unconscious as freely as possible, in whatever language or as many languages as you want to use.

Art: When your feelings can't be put into words, consider expressing yourself through art. Painting, drawing, sculpting, ceramics, crafts, singing, playing a musical instrument, dancing, cooking, baking, flower arranging, home decorating, sewing, gardening, or making collages are excellent emotional outlets. You don't need formal training in an art to express yourself. Once again, try not to judge your efforts—just let them give voice to what is in your heart.

Expressing yourself through art is a suggestion, not a requirement. You can combine artwork with your journal writing, or you can do them separately, as you wish.

A Final Note

This book is only a beginning guide to recovery from sexual assault. Its focus on improving your self-esteem by means of rational thinking provides the foundation you will need to address the impact of the sexual assault on the areas of your life not addressed in this book, such as your career, communication skills, sexuality, creativity, spirituality, and relationships.

Remember that no self-help book, regardless of its quality, is a substitute for individual, couples, or family counseling. You probably will need the assistance of a qualified health professional, and perhaps a spiritual advisor, to support and strengthen your recovery efforts.

Although sexual assault can leave long-lasting psychic and physical scars, many survivors have rebuilt their lives. Some even credit the assault with forcing them to take better care of themselves and to look closer at their priorities. Many survivors before you have restored their sense of personal power and made positive changes in their lives. So can you.

Note: Because women are the primary victims of sexual assault, this book is addressed to women. This is not intended to minimize the harsh reality that men are also sexually assaulted.

CHAPTER 1

Getting Ready

Walking the Tightrope:
The Dilemma of the Healing Process

Sometimes your journey to recovery will feel smooth and safe. Other times, you will feel as though you are standing on a psychic tightrope, precariously perched between two opposing but equally compelling forces. One force beckons you to walk forward, toward recovery, while the other frantically warns you to go no further, lest you lose your balance and fall into the abyss of an emotional or mental chaos from which you may never return.

This pull toward recovery and its opposite, the warning to stop, are both normal responses to assault and they both have the same goal—self-preservation. The desire for recovery comes from your inborn need to grow, your awareness that unless you confront the memories of your assault, they will continue to poison your life for years to come. The warning to stop derives from another inborn need, the need for safety. A part of your psyche wants to protect you from the potentially destabilizing emotions you are likely to experience when you revisit the assault with all of its pain and horror.

If you experience such a tug-of-war while you are working with this book, you need to recognize it for what it is: the normal ambivalence experienced by survivors when they contemplate what they may face during their recovery process. Do not be ashamed of this ambivalence and do not interpret it as meaning that you don't want to, don't need to, or might never, recover.

Sometimes the fear, numbness, anger, or physical pain you might feel while working with this book may seem more intense than the feelings you experienced during the assault itself. Do not misinterpret that, either. There are good reasons for this. During the assault, your body was producing various biochemical forms of anesthesia to help dull the shock and impact of the attack. You may have experienced severe physical and emotional pain during the assault; however, your sufferings would have been even greater without the various neurohormones provided by nature to buffer the blows of fate.

Now you are facing examining the trauma without these buffers. But do not despair. There are proven ways of structuring the healing process so as to minimize the distress inherent in reviewing one of the worst experiences of your life.

For instance, you don't have to review every single detail or feel every possible feeling associated with the assault to recover. You need to recall only enough of what happened and experience only enough of what you felt then, so that you can understand why you are so unhappy. Furthermore, you don't have to endure the pangs of recovery alone. You can learn how to find safe people who will listen to you and support you. The first four chapters of this book are intended to guide you in creating the necessary safeguards so you can revisit the past with the least disruption to your present as is possible.

Your Basic Rights

You have the right to spend quality time on yourself; to decide how long and how often you want to work with this book; to choose those with whom you will share your recovery and how much, where, and when you will share; to create a safe, comfortable, and nurturing environment in which to work on your healing; and to ask for help from friends, therapists, and family members. Most importantly, you have the right to change your mind about any of these decisions when they no longer feel comfortable to you.

How Long Will You Work with This Book?

You had no control over when your assault began or when it ended. However, you can control when to begin and end your recovery work sessions. Establishing safe time limits will help to protect you from becoming overwhelmed. In general, it is recommended that you not work with this book more than half an hour at a time. But neither is half an hour work session mandatory. The time frame is your choice. It is also recommended to set a timer or find another way to remind yourself when you reach your time limit.

Now, stop reading and close your eyes for a while. Form a mental image of yourself using this book. Reflect on how long you think you could tolerate focusing on the assault at one sitting, and about the demands on your time that are essential and cannot be neglected.

Then open your eyes and in your journal answer these questions: (1) "How long *can* I work with this book at a time?" and (2) "How long do I *want* to work with it?" You may want to stay with it longer than you think you can or vice versa. Of the two time periods you selected, the *shorter* one should set the *outer* limit for your work sessions. Review your decision again. Is the time frame you are choosing realistic in terms of your lifestyle and your emotional needs?

You need to work with this book at least once or twice a week in order to maintain your focus on recovery. Working with it more often than twice a week is not recommended because you need time in between work sessions to absorb and reflect upon what you have discovered about your experience. If you are in a survivors group or in individual therapy, the decision about how often you need to work with this book should be discussed with your group leader or therapist.

If you choose a time period such as twenty minutes, don't worry that this is "not enough." What ever *you* decide is enough is enough. The fact that you are willing to revisit such a painful trauma is heroic in itself.

Much can be accomplished in twenty minutes. You can read a section and glance at the accompanying questions without answering them. At your next session, you can begin to answer them, stopping after twenty minutes, even if you haven't finished.

If twenty minutes a session is all you can take, then take as many twenty-minute sessions as you need to complete a particular exercise.

Also, you don't always have to read or write about new material. Reviewing what you have already read or written will help you to digest and process your efforts on a deeper level. More can be gained by working slowly, safely, and thoroughly, than by speeding through the book mechanically in the desire to "get it over with" and to "be normal" as soon as possible.

After a few sessions, experiment with your time limit a few times, then evaluate it. Is too long or too short? Too frequent or not frequent enough? If you decide to make a change, consider the change an experiment. Try it out, then decide if it was helpful. If not, experiment with another time frame until you find one that works for you.

Making Time for Your Healing

Just as you would not expect yourself to function at an optimal level while recuperating from a major illness, you cannot expect yourself to be as efficient and productive as you were in the past. *Temporarily,* your life will not be as balanced either, because during the healing process, your energies will be directed inward, not outward. At first, the results of your efforts may not be visible. But that doesn't mean you aren't working hard. Eventually, the positive results of your inner work will be evident.

Healing requires effort, thought, concentration, and that most precious of all commodities: time. First, you need to identify your essential responsibilities and then be willing to let go of all the rest. To counteract the emotionally draining effects of working with this book, you also will need to set aside time to replenish yourself by taking naps or walks, sharing with friends, or doing whatever nurtures you. If for financial or other reasons it is impossible for you to take time away from your commitments, you may need to work with this book more slowly. Simplifying your life can also be helpful. (See appendix B, Resources, for suggested readings.)

As you contemplate clearing your schedule to make time for healing, you may wonder whether you are being selfish. Others may even tell you that you are being selfish. If this is the case, you need to say the following sentences aloud ten times or write them ten times in your journal: "Taking care of myself is not self-ish. I need and deserve this time for healing." Another way to encourage yourself is to say "I love myself" ten times, or write it ten times in your journal. You might also look at a picture of yourself while repeating this affirmation aloud.

A Matter of Life and Death

Now you might be thinking, "But I can't make time for all that! I have a job, children, other responsibilities!" However, have you considered these questions: How many hours a week do you spend feeling anxious, sad, or half-alive because of the assault? How many hours of sleep, joy, and productive work have you lost?

Add to this the number of hours you may have spent over-eating, drinking, drugging, or overspending because of the assault. How many hours and how much money have you lost recuperating from such episodes all the while berating yourself for these behaviors? Now, add to that total the hours you estimate you will spend thinking about and reacting to the assault over the next ten years.

How many hours is that? Are you willing to spend a tenth of that time on recovery? If you had cancer and had to drive a hundred miles a day for treatment, you'd go. If you had to wait three hours to be seen, you'd wait. Nobody would call you "self-ish" for spending so much time on yourself because, after all, cancer is a matter of life and death.

Post-traumatic stress, depression, addiction, and the other common consequences of sexual assault can suppress the immune system; be high risk factors for diabetes, heart disease, hyper-tension, dermatological problems, the growth of tumors, and any number of bronchial conditions; contribute to premature death, complications after surgery, and the development of a life-threatening addiction; furthermore, they can lead to a greater probability of being physically or sexually attacked or economi-cally exploited in the future.

Think of the hours you will spend on healing as medical appointments for a very serious condition. This is not a mind game. It is the truth. It is also true that realistic demands on your time and unavoidable essential responsibilities can interfere with your commitment to healing. However, some obstacles may come from within you. Are you angry that you are still suffering and that you, not your assailant, are the one who has to spend time and money on recovery? If so, your anger is entirely justified, but you can't stop taking care of yourself. Not recovering will harm only you, not your attacker.

Or perhaps you hesitate to fully embrace the healing process because you want to punish your traumatized self for being helpless, victimized, and confused during the attack or acting in ways that you consider shameful. Yet the woman who was traumatized is still a part of you, and your instinct for self-preservation is not going to permit her knowledge and experience simply to disappear. Pushing her away, fighting, or ridiculing her won't make her disappear: these acts only use up psychic energy that you could be investing in your life today.

If you really want to reduce the influence of your traumatized self on your life, you need to get to know her and make friends with her, no matter how much you despise her or wish she were different. You can build a relationship with her the same way you'd build a relationship with any other person: you talk to that person and try to see her point of view.

One way to get to know your traumatized self is to write a letter to her and have her write a letter to you. Of course, you may need to write many letters or find other ways to converse with her. If you are seeing a therapist, gestalt techniques, such as talking to parts of yourself in session, might be very helpful.

Exercise: Write a Letter to Your Traumatized Self

Step 1: Letter to Your Traumatized Self

Imagine yourself during the assault. What did you look like? What were you wearing? Who were your friends? Where were you living? What were your hobbies? What did you think about? Holding an image of your traumatized self in your mind's eye, write a letter to her. Tell her how you feel about her. For example, here is Suzanne's first letter to her traumatized self:

Dear You,
I can't stand you. You're always whining about the assault.

People are sick of hearing about it, but no one is more sick of it than me. When he grabbed you, you just stood there like the wimpy crybaby you are. You should be ashamed of yourself. If you had tried harder, you could have escaped! You gave up then, so why bother trying to heal? You pathetic nothing. Therapy can't help you. It helps only a select few and you aren't one of them. You're a born loser. I'm a successful woman, and you, a self-pitying crybaby, are interfering with my career. I hate thinking about you and I hate this stupid exercise.

—Suzanne

Step Two: The Assault Survivor Replies

After you write the letter to your traumatized self, have that self write a letter back and continue the interaction. For example, Suzanne's assaulted self wrote back:

Dear Suzanne,
Thanks for talking to me. Hardly anyone wants to talk to me. They shrink away from me as if I have the plague. They feel contempt for me, as you do. You're right. I was too passive. I probably could have stopped him. But I didn't want to be passive, and I didn't want to be raped, either. I don't care what anyone says. I didn't like it. I hated it so much. I hate myself for being a woman. I wish you had been there when I was being tortured, for it was torture. You would have known how to get me out of it. But you weren't there. Nobody was. You're right, I deserve to be miserable. I'm just a bad person.

Step 3: Dialoguing

To get the most out of this exercise, you need to maintain a dialogue between yourself and your traumatized self. Try to write back and forth to each other as much as you can. For example, Suzanne replied to her traumatized self:

"You weren't bad. He was. He and our sexist society are to blame, not you. It could have happened to anyone. No woman deserves what happened to you, no matter how mixed up or imperfect she is. You aren't as ugly as I thought you were, either."

Then, her traumatized self wrote back: "Really? Can you help me now? Can you be there for me when I get those looks from others, and when I get scared that he'll come for me again? Can you help me to keep on trying no matter how alone and miserable I feel?"

Suzanne's response: "Yes, and I'll stop calling you names and hating you for being a woman."

By writing these letters, Suzanne came to see that the energy she spent loathing her sexually assaulted self would be better spent trying to protect and understand that part of herself.

If you cannot complete these dialoguing exercises, then do some writing about why you can't. Discussing this issue with a qualified therapist is highly recommended.

Rewards: Small and Large

After you've spent time with this book, congratulate yourself. Be proud that you've had enough self-love to begin to strengthen yourself. Every time you work with an exercise, reward yourself, as well.

A reward is something that gives you pleasure and satisfaction in itself, with little or no thought toward meeting a specific goal. It lifts you up and energizes you. This is the difference between reading a book for fun as opposed to reading it for an exam. Rewards also need to be safe. Indulging in substance abuse or a spending spree does not qualify as a reward.

If you feel you don't deserve a reward because you had a difficult time working with an exercise or because you think you haven't made much progress, reward yourself anyway. Are you angry that you have to reward yourself and that no one else is available or willing to do that for you? Nurture yourself in spite of these feelings. Don't put off giving to yourself until you have done "enough" or until you are so depleted that you have no choice but to give to yourself.

Each time you reward yourself, you affirm that your healing matters. Some part of you knows you are a valuable person; otherwise you would not choose to heal. No reward, regardless how small, is insignificant. Each act of self-love is a healthy way of fighting back. No excuses allowed! There are dozens of free activities that take less than five minutes that can serve as rewards. If you want more than five-minute rewards, take them. What you choose is not as important as actually following through with this idea. (For helpful books, see appendix B.)

Exercise: Small Rewards

Think about some small realistic ways you could reward yourself after each work session. One suggestion is to spend five minutes longer on enjoyable activities that are already a part of your life. For example, take a shower, prepare a favorite meal, meet a friend, read, garden, exercise, or listen to music. The spiritually inclined may find that deeper study of spiritual texts is rewarding. For some people, keeping a prayer journal is rewarding.

However, you will need to screen out any rewards that remind you of negative experiences, especially of the assault. For example, if you were forced to take a shower by the assailant, rewarding yourself with a long, hot shower clearly will not work for you.

Create a page in your journal with the title "Small Rewards." Then list at least ten small ways you can reward yourself for your work with this book. When one of your choices no longer feels rewarding, pick another one from your list.

Large Rewards

When you feel as if you've had a major breakthrough in your recovery or when you've just emerged from a period of enormous pain, it's time to give yourself a big reward. Large rewards do not have to be expensive. They can be free, like a picnic in a local park, or relatively inexpensive, like visiting a museum or renting a favorite video. A large reward is participating in any activities that are fun to do, or nurturing, and, most of all, safe. As with small rewards, what you give yourself is far less important than the fact that you give yourself something. The only requirement is that your choice promotes either your physical, emotional, or spiritual well-being.

Exercise: Large Rewards

In your journal create a page entitled "Large Rewards," then write down at least five rewards that you would consider "large." If you draw a blank, think of that special girl whom you want to shower with love to help her heal. What might she enjoy doing? Would you enjoy something similar?

Creating Your Own Safe and Special Place

If the assault punctured your self-esteem, you may feel that you don't deserve a safe, quiet, and nurturing place to work with this book and take your healing seriously. But you do deserve to heal, and creating your own healing place is part of the healing process. You can create your own personal temple, which you enter with the specific purpose of healing yourself.

You can set aside a specific spot in your home to be your healing space. The seating, lighting, and temperature need to be comfortable. Make this place uniquely yours by decorating it as you wish or by placing photographs, artwork, or other items of personal importance. Provide soothing music if you wish. Alternatively, you could work with this book during your therapy sessions or in a trusted friend's home; your healing space could be in your backyard or garden, or your church, temple, or synagogue. Any place where you feel safe and comfortable, and can be free from interruptions will do.

Using Mirrors

If you have negative associations with mirrors, ignore any suggestions that involve them. However, if mirrors are free of bad memories, looking at yourself in the mirror while you say aloud, "I deserve healing," can increase the power of this self-affirmation.

Establishing Privacy

Have you ever been told that a person is as "sick as their secrets" or that "spilling your guts" will free you? Being pressured by well-meaning others or by pop-psychology platitudes about "getting it all out" when you don't want to or are afraid can feel similar to the assault, where you didn't have the right to say no.

Furthermore, there is no evidence that forcing people to reveal some of the most painful and humiliating moments of their lives is of any benefit in itself. In fact, it can create even stronger feelings of shame and inferiority.

You have the right to as much privacy as you need. You don't have to talk about any aspect of the assault or your recovery with anyone unless you choose to do so. Trust your inner voice. If something within you says "Stop" when you are writing in your journal or sharing with others, then stop. You can always continue later on in your journey to recovery.

Exercise: Your Privacy

In your journal, create a new page entitled "My Privacy." Then, describe how you will maintain the privacy of your journal or any artwork you may make as part of your recovery. Will they safe out in the open? Do they need to be locked in a container or entrusted to a dependable person for safekeeping?

Now write the following sentence five times: "I have the right to as much privacy as I want." You can repeat this statement out loud a few times, as well.

Contract: Promises to Yourself

You are now ready to put together all the decisions you have made thus far about how you will go about working with this book. In your journal, create a page called "Contract: Promises to Myself." Then, to review your work thus far, write out the following paragraph, inserting the answers to questions in the parentheses from your answers to the exercises you completed earlier in this chapter. As you review your answers, ask yourself whether they reflect your choices, the expectations of others, or old unhealthy habits. Feel free to add more specific details to amend whatever you wish.

This contract is your commitment to yourself to recover and heal from your assault. Are you willing to do this for yourself? You may find it helpful to read this contract before each work session or if you become discouraged along the way. Reading it to others and having them affirm your resolve can also be helpful. You also may want to practice forming a mental image of yourself gently working with the exercises in this book or helping someone you love who deserves extra-special care—yourself.

Contract: Promises to Myself

I owe it to myself to help myself heal because (list at least three reasons). Not only I, but the people who matter most to me will benefit from my recovery. The best form of revenge for the injustice of being attacked is to make my life the most fulfilling that it can be.

It's best for me to work with this book _____ times a _____ for _____ minutes at a time, and not a minute longer. I will increase this time only if it feels safe, and only if I set new limits on my time commitment. I will try not to judge my efforts as not good enough or to berate myself if I am unable to stick to this schedule.

I plan to write in my journal/do my artwork at (specify location) and to protect it by (list the measures you will take to maintain privacy). I will also respect all messages from my inner self warning me that I need to hold back from writing or thinking about particular incidents or emotions or from sharing my thoughts with others, even if they sincerely want to help me.

I will not work with this book when I am under stress from fatigue, hunger, my illness or the illness of a family member, a family crisis, or urgent responsibilities. Also, I will not work with this book if no one is available to support me, should I need immediate support.

Signed: _____

The Importance of Checking In

Checking in with yourself is an act of self-affirmation, a way of reminding yourself that your inner being matters. It is also a way of giving yourself credit for all your efforts. At the end of each chapter, you will be asked to check in with yourself by answering specific questions. You can also check in with yourself any other time you might feel disturbed by the work you will be doing with this book.

Directions for Checking In

Begin a new page in your journal entitled "My Reactions to Chapter (fill in the chapter number)," and answer the following questions:

- What are you thinking right now? How are you feeling? Empowered, drained, frightened, ashamed, hopeful, angry, or some other feeling? What physical discomforts are you experiencing?

- Do you need to take a break to comfort and stabilize yourself? Do you want to contact a safe friend, or do something else to take care of yourself emotionally, physically, or mentally?

- What have you learned in working with this chapter?

- How do you feel about the work you have completed?

- Have you honored the contracts you set for yourself in this (and other) chapters?

- Have you remembered to reward yourself?

- Is it safe to share your progress and concerns with someone you trust?

Answer all of the questions to the best of your ability and feel free to ask and answer additional questions if you wish.

CHAPTER 2

Your Physical Health and Safety

Has the assault caused you to dislike or disregard your body? If so, this is a common and understandable reaction to being sexually attacked. But you don't have to treat your body the way your attacker did. He tried to destroy its dignity and strength. Don't you complete the job! Don't attack yourself by neglecting your physical health. Take loving care of your body with proper nutrition, rest, exercise, and any needed medical care.

Taking of Care of Your Physical Health

If you dread medical appointments, you are not alone. Many rape survivors are reluctant to seek medical care because of certain similarities between medical appointments and sexual assault. These similarities can revive memories of the assault, leading to flashbacks, anxiety, depression, or other forms of distress.

Like sexual assault, medical appointments can involve disrobing; physical pain or the possibility of pain; and being relatively passive while another person touches you and perhaps inserts something into your body. Medical offices may remind you of being attacked behind closed doors or confined, trapped, or locked in a space with no escape. Under anesthesia, you are helpless, just as you were during the assault.

Even if you have no visible injuries, you may feel that being assaulted "shows," and that therefore you'll be shamed or mistreated by a medical worker. Needing treatment for any assault-related injuries can easily remind you of the injustice and cruelty you have endured. Perhaps you have had negative experiences in medical facilities in the past or have heard about other rape survivors being humiliated or even propositioned by medical staff.

The good news, however, is that increasing numbers of medical professionals are learning about sexual assault and its aftermath, and they sincerely want to be sensitive to survivors' needs. The following suggestions can help you arrange medical visits so you will feel more in control.

Tips to Reduce the Stress of Medical and Dental Appointments

1. Except for urgent medical matters, such as testing for sexually transmitted diseases (STDs), avoid making appointments close to the anniversary date of the assault.

2. If the doctor's office or clinic is located near the site of the assault or near another reminder, try to get medical help at a different location.

3. If waiting increases your anxiety, ask for the first appointment in the morning or after lunch.

4. If arriving early helps you by giving you time to relax, go early.

5. Whatever time you go, bring along a book or magazine, your journal, a cassette player so you can listen to music or a book on tape, a snack or beverage, pictures of your loved ones, or anything else that might help you feel more comfortable while you are waiting for your appointment.

6. Ask a friend or relative to go with you or arrange to meet or talk with one later.

7. If you want a female staff member to be present, ask if this is possible, if not for the entire visit, at least for part of it.

8. If you prefer a female doctor, find out if this an option.

9. Put all your questions in writing beforehand. That way you won't forget any of them. Perhaps a friend, a mental health professional, a member of the clergy, or a teacher can help you with this and agree to be available by phone if the doctor has questions.

   Ask about the length and nature of the consultation and any examinations or procedures that will be involved; the tests that will be given and why; the instruments to be used; who will be in the room with you; and the kinds of physical discomfort you can expect during or after your visit. Inquire about all options. During the assault, you had few options. Today you need to know all of your options, even if you never use them.

10. Take notes on the replies to your questions.

11. If anesthesia is suggested, ask whether it is really needed. How much pain might you experience without it, and is it medically feasible or advisable to begin the procedure without anesthesia, and be given some later on, if the pain becomes unbearable?

12. If you can take a break during the appointment or leave when you think you can't stand another minute, you will feel less trapped and more in control. However, these options may or may not be medically possible or advisable. You won't know unless you ask.

13. You don't have to mention or discuss the assault unless you choose to. You only have to ask and answer relevant questions and state what you need.

14. Provide the doctor's office with the names and phone numbers of persons to call in case you need support or to be taken home.

15. If a doctor or clinic is not supportive, shop around for a new one. If your insurance plan or financial resources make this impossible, ask others to help you figure out ways to meet your medical needs.

"What If It's All in My Head?"

"First I had pains in my chest. The tests showed nothing. Then the pains moved to my stomach, then to my back, then to my knees. Each time, the doctors found nothing. Now my ears are ringing, but I won't go for testing. If I go and they don't find anything again, then I'll know I'm crazy. Everyone in my family thinks I'm a hypochondriac anyway," says Maria.

Have you, like Maria, been told you that your physical problems are "all in your head?" Does a part of you believe this, as well? Is this why you hesitate to seek medical care? If so, you need to rethink your decision. Your life may depend on it.

Despite the amazing progress of medical science, there are still many unknowns. Experts agree that some physical ailments that seem to have a psychological origin may have a physiological basis as well, one that has yet to be officially recognized or discovered.

Always seek medical attention for any bleeding, pain, or physical irregularity. Even if some of your symptoms are stress-related, that doesn't mean they aren't real, that they don't have some physical basis, or that nothing can alleviate them. Furthermore, you never know when physical discomfort is the signal for a serious medical problem.

Exercise: Take Care of Your Body

In your journal, list of all your medical concerns. Don't leave anything out, not even problems you think are "minor" or "all in your head." Consider the following suggestions:

Complete physicals. If you haven't had one recently, get one. Find out when you will need one in the future.

Gynecological visits. Gynecological physicians can detect internal scarring, STDs, and other problems that can contribute to infertility and a host of other health problems. In recent years there have been many advances in treating scar tissue. Scars are daily reminders of the rape. Gynecologists, like dermatologists, may be able to recommend ways to make any external scars less visible. Making them less obvious can help promote your peace of mind.

Testing for STDs. If there is even a remote possibility that you contracted an STD, get to a doctor or clinic immediately. Be sure to be tested for chlamydia, gonorrhea, syphilis, and herpes simplex virus, as well as the HIV virus and any other STDs that your doctor recommends. Of all the medical appointments, testing for STDs can create the most fear (and anger). Do not procrastinate. Early treatment of an STD can save your life.

Dental visits. If you were forced to perform oral sex or to eat or swallow something unpleasant, you may be reluctant to see a dentist. But letting your teeth deteriorate won't harm your abuser one bit, only you.

Review your list of medical concerns and prioritize them. (If possible, obtain medical help with this.) Then rewrite your list in rank order. Put the most important medical concern first, and the least important last. Leave two or three lines in between each entry.

Stop working with this book right now and go find the phone numbers of the doctors or clinics you need for each medical condition. If you need to obtain a list of providers or authorization from your insurance company to see a doctor, do so. Inquire about coverage for complementary medical treatments, especially for acupuncture.

If your health plan seems inadequate to meet your needs, shop around for a better one. If you do not have insurance, call a local hospital, your county government, a sexual assault center, or local medical and dental schools for information about free or low-cost medical services.

Return to your journal and for each health concern, write the following: the names and phone numbers of the doctors or clinics you need to reach, the time period within which you will call for an appointment, the time period within which you will try to schedule an appointment, and your commitment to keeping the appointment.

For example, "Medical issue #1: Dental work. Dr. _____, phone number: _____ . I will call the office by _____ (date) and try to make an appointment within _____ (specify time period). I commit to keeping this appointment."

Very Important Note: As soon as possible, ask a qualified medical professional to review your list of medical concerns. Based on her or his advice, you may need to reprioritize or add to your list. You may also discover that you can remove something from your list.

Exercise: Improve Your Living Environment

Your living environment needs to be as safe as possible. In this section, you will examine your living situation for any unsafe areas that can be improved. Create a new page in your journal entitled "A Safe Living Environment," and answer the following questions:

1. How safe is your residence? Are there adequate locks and other needed safeguards on the windows and doors? Do you keep them locked at appropriate times? Are there any electrical or other structural problems, such as a leaky roof, flooded basement, falling ceiling, or faulty gas heater that need attention?

   Do you have smoke alarms, fire extinguishers, or a security system? Do you check them as prescribed to be sure they are in working order? Are there any other safety problems in your residence that need attention?

2. How can you make your residence as safe as possible? Consider installing a security system, joining a neighborhood watch group, or getting a dog. Also, get to know your neighbors. If you live alone, would you feel safer with a roommate, provided the roommate was safe and had safe habits and friends? If you live with people who are lax about security, whom you don't trust, who have unsafe habits such as drinking and drugging, or who have friends you don't think are safe, it may be time to discuss your safety needs with your roommates. If there is no improvement, consider finding a new roommate or another place to live.

   It is not uncommon for assault survivors to move to another location if their attacker lives in the neighborhood; if he has threatened to return; or if they were attacked in their home and need to get away from the memories. You will need to weigh the pros and cons of such a decision. If you do relocate, do not denigrate your decision by viewing it as "letting him win." It is your way of taking control and protecting yourself.

3. How safe is your vehicle? Is your insurance coverage adequate? Are the brakes, tires, and other parts in good

working order? Do you use your seat belts faithfully? What steps can you take to make sure your vehicle is as safe as possible?

4. Do you have xeroxed copies of your credit cards, driver's license, bank account numbers, and other important financial and legal papers in case they are lost or stolen?

5. Do you have unprotected sex, associate with persons with histories of or tendencies toward violence, or walk in high-crime areas without taking proper precautions? Are there other ways you flirt with death? Can you commit to stopping these or any other behaviors that jeopardize your life? If you can't make that commitment or you find that, despite your commitment, you are unable to keep yourself safe, seek professional help immediately.

6. Do you own a weapon or live in a household that has guns, explosives, or other such weapons? Are these weapons registered and securely locked? If you feel unsafe due to these weapons, are there any steps you can take to be safer?

7. If you are currently living in a violent or abusive home or work situation, you need to seek professional, legal, and other types of assistance immediately. Consult Appendix B for guidance.

8. Might an exercise or weight-lifting program or a self-defense class increase your physical strength and self-confidence? Many rape survivors have found that self-defense courses gave them an increased sense of control over their lives, as well as increased protection against future attacks. Check with your physician and therapist (if you have one) before you enroll in any of these activities. Also check out the qualifications of the instructors.

9. If you were attacked while jogging, do your jogging with others. If you were assaulted on campus, walk with others or ask the campus police to escort you. If you were assaulted in a parking garage and must use one again, park only within a few feet of the exit or if you have someone with you. Try to find a well-lit, safe alternative place to park.

Exercise: Your Medical and Mental Health Safety Plan

The more often you review your safety plan, the more it will become a part of you. Remember, you are learning new ways, and learning anything new, even something you want to learn, is hard.

In your journal on a new page entitled "My Medical and Mental Health Safety Plan," write following paragraph, inserting your answers to the exercises you completed in this chapter. As you review your answers, ask yourself whether they reflect your choices, the expectations of others, or old unhealthy habits. Feel free to add more specifics or amend whatever you wish. Reading this contract to others and having them affirm the importance of taking care of your health also can be helpful.

My Medical and Mental Health Safety Plan

I commit to taking care of my health and making my living environment as safe as possible by following the plans I've made in this chapter. More specifically,

I commit to making appointments for the following medical problems by the dates specified. (List each problem and the goal date for seeking care.)

If I have any of the reactions listed under "Cautions" in the introduction, I will follow the suggestions in that section. If at any time I feel suicidal, homicidal, very frightened, out of touch with reality, or out of control in any manner, I will stop working with this book immediately and call a local sexual assault center, a crisis hot line, my therapist, or another qualified mental health professional.

(Write down the names and phone numbers of your local sexual assault center, your therapist or survivors group leader, three qualified mental health professionals, and three hot lines here. You need several contacts to help assure that at least one of them will be available if needed. Consult appendixes A and B for information on locating a therapist, a sexual assault center, and local hot lines.)

If I need to go to an emergency room, these are the hospitals I can go to (list the names and phone numbers of three local hospitals here).

If I am currently being physically, sexually, or emotionally abused, I will take steps to free myself, beginning with consulting with a qualified mental health professional.

I commit to making the following changes in my living situation and personal habits to insure my safety: (review your answers to the exercise "Improve Your Living Environment" to answer this question).

I commit to this contract because my life is worth saving and in this life I deserve some happiness and peace of mind.

Signed _____

Checking in: Return to the "Directions for Checking In" at the end of chapter 1, and answer all the questions to the best of your ability.

CHAPTER 3

Building a Human Safety Net

You may have endured the assault alone, but you do not have to recover alone. You will heal faster and with less struggle if you have people in your life who can help comfort you when you are hurting, remind you of your progress when you feel discouraged, serve as reality checks when you feel confused, and rejoice with you as you grow stronger. These supportive relationships also can help protect you from developing long-term negative reactions to the assault. Many women experience some depression, increased anxiety, insomnia, or other post-traumatic symptoms shortly after being sexually assaulted. For some, these symptoms begin to fade after a month. For others, however, the symptoms persist.

When symptoms last for more than a month, a vicious cycle can begin. The symptoms are not only troublesome in themselves, but if they persist, they then go on to create even more problems, for example, relationship, self-esteem, and job-related problems, which, in turn, usually cause the symptoms to become more frequent or more severe. As the symptoms worsen, so do the survivor's problems functioning in relationships or on the job. This process can continue until a crisis is precipitated, which is why it is called a vicious cycle.

For some survivors, those who have people who love and support them, this vicious cycle never starts. Research has repeatedly found that women who are able to retain a sense of belonging to their family or to others certainly do suffer the aftereffects of assault. However, they are less likely to develop long-term reactions when compared to those who feel alienated from their family or others. Furthermore, survivors who have supportive relationships tend to recover faster and the results of their therapeutic efforts tend to be more long-lasting (van der Kolk, McFarlane, and Weisaeth 1996).

Self-sufficiency is important, but it isn't everything. If the assault damaged some of your important relationships and you now feel like an outcast, it is all the more essential that you find new people who can give you the support that everyone needs to survive. Like it or not, we humans are biologically programmed to need comfort and to be energized by human contact.

"Pain is needy: it longs to be understood" (Datcher 2001, 17). However, your companions must be carefully selected. Unkind, critical people must be avoided. You also need to avoid those who believe that talking about suffering is a sign of weakness. The exercises in this chapter will guide you in deciding with whom it might be safe to be open and honest. Although there is no surefire method for selecting trustworthy, caring friends, there are ways of making the best possible choices.

If you already have friends, you are fortunate. If you don't, building your human safety net will take some time and effort. In our age of tight schedules and geographic mobility, it isn't always easy to make friends. If, after the assault, some of the people important to you became critical or distant, finding new friends might be painful to you. As you meet new people, you may remember those who are no longer as loving to you as they used to be.

Building a support system may be especially difficult if you grew up in an abusive setting. Most likely your childhood perpetrator tried to isolate you. You may have learned "not to tell" and to monitor your words and deeds carefully in the hope of avoiding the perpetrator's anger. You may not have been adequately parented, either. Perhaps you acted as a parent to your parent, rather than the other way around, while simultaneously trying to nurture and protect your siblings or others. If that was the case, then trusting others might feel unfamiliar, if not downright dangerous. For you, ideas like asking for help and depending on others to actually come through for you may seem like fairy tales from another planet. It will take time for you to feel safe sharing with others.

You may encounter similar difficulties in trusting others if one or more of your caretakers suffered from a substance abuse problem or an untreated psychiatric disorder. Be patient with yourself and seek help for this problem. Professional help also may be needed.

Identifying Supportive Others

In the past, staying silent may have been an excellent survival skill. However, the opposite extreme, that is, telling everyone about the assault and your feelings, is not recommended. Your goal now is to be selective about whom you turn to for help. The following exercise can help you identify persons who, on the basis of what you know now, are "safe."

If, while completing this exercise, you discover that you know only one or two supportive persons, do not despair. Even if you can think of no one you can trust, do not give up hope. You can build a support system, one person at a time. A good place to begin is by finding a therapist or joining a sexual assault survivors group. (See appendix A for suggestions on finding a therapist and survivors groups.)

Survivor chat rooms on the Internet, although potential sources of support, are not recommended. There are no built-in protections on these sites, making you vulnerable to the feedback of persons whom you do not know. Anyone can participate in these chat rooms, including those with severe mental illnesses, voyeurs, and sexual predators.

Exercise: Identifying Supportive Others

In your journal, answer the following questions:

1. With whom do I *not* feel safe sharing about my assault and my work with this book? Write the names of at least

five persons. You can write more names if necessary. For each person, list at least one reason why you don't feel safe with her or him. Even if you don't have a clear reason, but instinctively sense that it isn't wise to talk to her or him, put that person on your "no" list. Remember, you are in charge. You get to make the rules about whom you talk to, and how much to reveal.

2. With whom *do* you feel safe sharing? List at least five persons with whom you feel safe. List more people if you want to, but not more than twelve. In general, it is difficult to maintain emotional intimacy with more than a dozen persons. For each person, answer the following questions:

3. What is it about this person that causes you to trust her or him?

4. How much does this person know about sexual assault and trauma?

5. Is this person comfortable talking about emotions or does she or he deny and fear them?

6. Does this person really listen? Does she or he wait for you to finish saying what you need to say before offering advice or feedback?

7. Does this person seem to accept and care for you, or do you feel she or he judges you?

8. Is this person trustworthy in some ways and untrustworthy in other ways?

9. How available is this person to support you? Does she or he have an untreated emotional or physical problem, such as substance abuse or chronic pain? Is she or he burdened with major health, financial, or family problems? Even if this person loves you dearly, given the realities of her or his life, to what degree can you count on this person to be there for you?

10. What would your relationship with this person be like if you had not been assaulted?

11. After answering all of the above questions, do you still feel this person could support you as you heal? If so, are there some aspects of the sexual assault or your present healing efforts that you would rather not share with this person? What areas are those?

Review your list. Cross off the names of any people who really don't feel safe, but whom you feel you should include because they have been helpful to you, because they are authority figures, or because you care about them, unless they meet the criteria specified in questions 3 through 11.

If you aren't sure: When in doubt about whether or not an individual is safe, think of a woman or girl whom you cherish who was sexually assaulted. Would she think this person is safe? If yes, why? If no, why not? If you still aren't sure, try writing a double dialogue between yourself as you are today and your traumatized self. Conducting a double dialogue is similar to writing a letter to your traumatized self and having that self respond (as in chapter 1). Even if you can't come to a decision, you will achieve greater clarity about why you feel so confused about this person.

Exercise: Safe List of Supportive People

Start a new page in your journal entitled "Safe People." Write the names and phone numbers of those persons whom you would feel comfortable calling in a time of need. If, in the future, you find that one of these persons is no longer helpful to you, take her or his name off your list. Add new safe persons as you find them. If there are certain conditions you want to remember, list those after the person's name. For example: Susan S. (phone number), Best time to call is _____ . Okay to talk about the assault, but not about _____ .

Keep a copy of this phone list handy, for example, in your purse or car, or near your telephone, provided these locations preserve your privacy. If want to leave a personal message on a friend's answering service, be sure to inquire about who else has access to their messages. If you want to use email, make certain that no one else has access to your email account, or to your friend's account, before you add your friend's email address to your list.

When you leave a message, be clear about your needs. Do not assume others will automatically know you are expecting a return call or that the matter is urgent. If you call a therapist or doctor's office, the same rules apply. If you want a callback or it is an emergency situation, say so. If you are working with a physician or other helping professional, inquire about who covers for them when they are not available. If they don't have adequate coverage, consider finding another therapist or physician.

What If No One Returns Your Calls?

In a perfect world, you wouldn't have to ask for help; the help would just arrive exactly when you needed it and in just the right way. But many times you will have to actively seek help, and when you find it, it will not be perfect. Suppose that during a particularly difficult moment, you reach out to someone on your safe list and that person is not available or attentive, or, even worse, that person is rejecting or critical of how you feel. What will you do?

You have every right to want help during a difficult time. Yet the hard truth is that no one is obligated to take care of you. The love and concern others give to you is a gift; hopefully, one you will receive in abundance in your life. However, except for scheduled group therapy, twelve-step meetings, and therapists who can reasonably be expected to be available, no one can be expected to be there for you every time you need someone in the exact manner that you desire. Even people who are devoted to you have their own lives to lead and their own pain to assuage. As important as you may be to them, at times something else may be their top priority, not you.

What is important here, however, is that when you reach out for support, you are affirming that you deserve it and that your emotional well-being is important to you. Others' undesirable reactions are not reflections of your worth. Consider their responses to you as valuable information about their reliability and availability and about the kinds of issues that are or are not comfortable for both of you to discuss. *Do not continue to ask for help from people who repeatedly have proved to be unreliable or unsupportive.*

Some survivors find it humbling, if not humiliating, to reach out to others. In our society, asking for help is frequently viewed as a sign of weakness. In the words of one survivor, "I hate needing." Today, women, especially professional women, are increasingly expected to act as if they were as "fiercely independent" as men supposedly are. But no one is totally independent. A close look at the lives of people who claim to be completely self-reliant will reveal that they need others to survive just like everyone else does.

If someone you turn to for help disappoints you, that hurts. You either can discuss the matter with that person or let it go. There is no one best way to handle such situations. But there are some wrong ways: harming others or yourself, indulging in an addiction, or destroying property. Talking about your reactions or writing in your journal are far healthier responses. (See appendix B for books on anger management and addiction.)

Minority Women

In the view of African-American writer Tracy Robinson (2000), some African-American women may find it exceptionally difficult to ask for help. A major reason for this, she writes, is that, historically, African-American women have been expected to be pillars of strength for others in the face of slavery, racism, and other oppressions. For many, this expectation still persists today.

However, time does not heal all wounds. If your culture defines "staying strong" as ignoring your personal needs, you may need to reconsider this definition of "staying strong." If you do not attend to your symptoms, they will only worsen. Eventually, they will interfere with your ability to be there for others, perhaps dramatically. Getting help is a way of regaining whatever degree of personal power you lost during the assault.

Don't Wait: Anticipate

Some survivors wonder how often to call or ask for help. You don't have to figure this out alone. Can you discuss this issue with a friend and decide how often or in what ways it works for both of you to be in touch with one another? Although you can't anticipate every emotional crisis, you can predict some of them. For example, you can expect to feel especially distressed on the anniversary of the assault, before or after an assault-related court hearing, or when you are in close proximity to the location of the assault.

But don't wait until you are so afraid that you are trembling or so depleted that you don't have the energy to pick up the phone. Take Benjamin Franklin's advice: An ounce of prevention is worth a pound of cure. *Plan for extra support around times and situations that you anticipate will bring up painful memories.*

There is, however, no "rule" that says you must reach out every time you are in pain. There may be times when you sense that talking about a problem might only make it worse. Other times, you may feel so vulnerable that your instinct may be to hide, not share. You may fear that if you reach out to someone, and that person says the wrong thing, you might be pushed into even deeper despair. Only you can decide which is less painful—being alone with your agony or taking the chance that someone's responses to you might add to your sorrow.

Relationships with Other Survivors

When you meet or read about other survivors whose assault seems much worse than yours, you might decide that you should forget about recovery and count your blessings instead. According to Shay "Placing one's self in a 'hierarchy of suffering' to one's own disadvantage is widespread among trauma survivors" (2002, 79). But there will always be women who are worse off than you. Even if another woman suffered more injuries than you did, you are entitled to grieve for your own pain, every bit of it. You are important, too, and you owe it to yourself to recover as much as possible. If at some point you want to help others, the more recovery you have, the more insight and courage you will have to share.

Jealousy is another feeling you may encounter. "Why is she (another survivor) recovering so much faster than I am?" or "How come her assault was worse than mine, and she's almost normal, and I'm not?" or "How did she recover without any help but I need as much help as I can get?"

Stop! Comparing yourself unfavorably to other survivors is a form of self-abuse. Some people have a more emotionally or physically reactive central nervous system than do others. Therefore, they respond more intensely to emotional and physical pain, which can prolong their recovery. Such emotional reactivity may be the combined result of genetic inheritance, upbringing, or prior life experiences. Yet in our society, where myths like "nobody can hurt you unless you let them," are widespread, emotional sensitivity is often viewed as personal failing. Emotionally sensitive and emotionally expressive people are often devalued. If you are emotionally sensitive, your recovery may be more difficult than it is for certain others. But this does mean that you are deficient in any way.

Also, recovery is not an all-or-nothing phenomenon. A survivor with progress in one area may have problems in another. The one who seems "normal" may be hurting in ways you cannot see, may be in denial about some issues, or may not want to expose her issues for fear of burdening others. Furthermore, the degree of a woman's recovery is highly dependent on factors outside of herself that are part of her recovery environment: her financial status, her access to good medical and psychological care, the amount of emotional support in her life, and the severity of the current stresses in her life.

Exercise: Your Recovery Environment

On a new page in your journal entitled "My Recovery Environment," answer these questions: After the assault, did the people and groups important to you embrace you with open arms or did they shun you? Did you have access to good medical and psychological help, or did you receive no help, or even worse, bad help?

Are you as healthy as you were before the attack or do you now have physical problems that remind you of the assault on a daily basis or that prevent you from living your life as you want? How satisfied, frustrated, or humiliated were you by the way you were treated by the police and the legal system? Is your attacker behind bars or is he free?

Was your assault followed by positive events, such as a promotion at work, or did it set off a cascade of events that led to unemployment, divorce, or other losses? Was your attack followed by negative events unrelated to the assault, such as a severe illness or a death in your family, another assault, a robbery, or another trauma?

Overall, did you have a positive recovery environment or a negative one that complicated and prolonged your recovery? More severe and longer term post-traumatic reactions have been found among survivors who were physically injured, who testified in court, or who had little access to medical and psychological care (Ullman and Filipas 2001).

Checking in: Return to the "Directions for Checking In" at the end of chapter 1 and answer all the questions to the best of your ability.

CHAPTER 4

Coping Skills

Fight, Flight, Freeze, and Other Trigger Reactions

When human beings are faced with danger, their adrenal glands flood their bodies with either adrenaline or noradrenaline. Adrenaline energizes the body in the fight or flight mode; noradrenaline creates a freeze reaction, or the numbing of the body and the emotions. This freeze reaction also can be caused by the endogenous opioid system, one of the body's natural calming systems, which diminishes physical sensations and the intensity of emotional reactions.

As a result of these involuntary physiological reactions, during a sexual assault, the woman doesn't have the power to decide whether she is going to fight back, try to run (flight), or go limp (freeze). Her adrenal glands and neurohormones do. The same holds true when she is exposed to a reminder of the assault, also called a "trigger." When exposed to a trigger, even if she is safe, her body responds as if she is being attacked.

If she responds with an adrenaline surge, leading to a fight or flight reaction, she may experience symptoms such as the startle response, insomnia, anxiety, irritability, and increased nightmares and flashbacks. If she responds with a noradrenaline surge, she may have a numbing or freeze reaction. Or, she may alternate between the symptoms of fight or flight reactions and the symptoms of a freeze reaction.

Some symptoms, such as difficulty concentrating, memory problems, and shutting down of the immune system, sexuality, and digestion are common to both adrenaline and noradrenaline reactions. Experiencing any of these involuntary reactions when you are exposed to a trigger, such as working with this book, is to be expected.

Signs of anxiety. Common signs of anxiety include nausea; sweating; rapid heart beat; difficulties concentrating; rapid shallow breathing; rapid or slurred speech; racing or scattered thinking; hot and cold flashes, light-headedness or dizziness; tremors or shaking; fear of losing control, going crazy, or dying; fatigue and body aches, especially stomach- and headaches.

Signs of numbing. Signs of numbing, also called "dissociation," include difficulties moving and speaking; dozing off or sleeping when you aren't tired; disinterest in sex; frequent memory or concentration problems (such as forgetting appointments, what you or someone else just said, or details of the assault that usually are in the forefront of your mind) which are not caused by depression, fatigue, head injury, medication, or substance abuse; confusion; feelings of unreality, floating in the air, or being in a trance or dreamlike state; feeling like an observer rather than a participant in your own life; covering yourself, sucking your thumb or a blanket or other childlike behaviors; and feeling detached from your body, mind, or emotions, even to the point of feeling dead or like a robot.

Common triggers or reminders of the assault. These include anniversary dates (of the assault, a related court hearing, major ruptures in relationships, suicide attempts, or the onset of a severe posttraumatic reaction); colors, smells, tastes, people, places (textures, landscapes, or the shape, size, or structure of a room), things (food, furniture, or other material items), or aspects of nature or time (weather, seasons, or time of day) associated with the assault even if they were not part of the danger; and people similar to those involved in the assault in age, height, looks, tone of voice, or attitude.

Other triggers include being or feeling confined or out of control of a situation; having to depend on others; media presentations, conversations, books, or discussions about sex, sexual assault, or other forms of violence; sexual activity or sexualized situations; any strong emotion, even joy, but especially emotions similar to those experienced during the assault; contact with the assailant; or any current stressor, such as financial, relationship, work, or medical problems; increased crime or other neighborhood problems; increased threats of terrorism, war, pollution, and the like; witnessing or being involved in a current trauma (fire, crime); and even a slight increase in ordinary everyday hassles.

Coping with Trigger Reactions

Rape survivors usually respond to triggers with symptoms such as anxiety, panic, flashbacks, irritability, anger, feelings of helplessness and hopelessness, changes in sexual desire, social isolation, addiction and other forms of self-abuse, and memory and concentration problems. Symptoms of dissociation (to be described later in this chapter), and symptoms of post-traumatic stress disorder or clinical depression may also develop. (See chapter 6.)

The coping methods presented here can help you to manage some of your trigger reactions and potentially minimize some of them, but they cannot eliminate them. Once you've been traumatized by sexual assault, post-assault reactions are hard-wired into your brain because of their survival value. As much as you may loathe them, those adrenaline surges that make you so jumpy and anxious or angry, or those noradrenaline surges that dampen your life spirit, are your friends: they helped you to survive the assault.

Flashbacks, nightmares, and intrusive thoughts, which are called "reliving symptoms," also serve a purpose. Experts view them as the mind's way of discharging the enormous amount of energy generated by the body during the assault; as ways of releasing memories so traumatic they are stored in the brain differently than other memories; as the mind's way of reviewing the past in hope of "making it right" or to find ways to avoid future assault; and as ways of commemorating the assault (Shephard 2001). Because sexual assault is such a hidden crime, the symptoms serve to bear witness, screaming out that, "It did happen. It mattered a lot then, and it matters a lot now."

Some trigger reactions will be easier to manage than others. Some may almost disappear eventually, while others may remain a problem for many years. Although you can't rid yourself entirely of trigger reactions, you can learn to view them as normal reactions to sexual trauma rather than as monsters trying to ruin your life. During the assault, these reactions helped keep you alive. It is only when they persist in safe situations that they cause problems and are, therefore, seen as symptoms rather than as the lifesavers they are.

Holding onto this perspective is the most important step for diffusing their negative meaning and power. When you denigrate and demoralize yourself by viewing your symptoms as signs of moral or emotional weakness, as punishment for wrongdoing, or as evidence that you will never again be happy, you are only feeding the hormonal stress reactions that you despise.

Vicious Cycles

Managing the reliving of your symptoms is essential to your recovery. Left unchecked, your anxiety can create more anxiety; your anger, more anger; your numbing, more numbing; and your flashbacks, more flashbacks. Eventually these vicious cycles can result in your worst fear coming true, that your symptoms will grow to the point where they dominate your whole being.

These vicious cycles follow this sequence: They begin with exposure to a trigger. This stimulates an involuntary adrenaline or noradrenaline surge, either of which can lead to anxiety, anger, dissociation, or despair. The next part of the sequence is your response to your trigger reactions. Even if you know that they are entirely normal, you may condemn yourself for having them.

Furthermore, because trigger reactions feel similar, if not identical, to the ways you felt during the assault, your mind automatically concludes that the assault or another trauma is either going on right now or certainly will occur in the future. Such fears lead to the production of additional adrenaline or noradrenaline surges, which intensify your symptoms.

While you observe your control over your body and mind diminishing, you may become gripped with a terrible fear: What if you can't protect or take care of yourself? To make matters worse, since this fear is reminiscent of the fear you experienced during the assault, it can stimulate additional adrenaline or noradrenaline surges, thus perpetuating the cycle.

The Anxiety Cycle

Once people experience an adrenaline surge in response to a trigger and begin to notice that they are anxious, they can become anxious *about* being anxious. They fear that they won't be able to control their anxiety, and that it will grow so strong they won't be able to function. Or they fear that their anxiety means that something terrible is about to happen.

Such fears lead to additional adrenaline surges, which can increase anxiety to a level where symptoms such as confusion, forgetfulness, nausea, or headaches begin to develop. These symptoms themselves can generate even more anxiety about losing control, which lead to even more adrenaline surges, and so forth.

The Anger Cycle

Adrenaline surges are also a part of anger. A vicious cycle can begin for women who get angry at themselves for being angry. Perhaps they were taught that anger was unfeminine or sinful, or they fear that they won't be able to control their anger. When they get angry at themselves for being angry, however, this only releases more adrenaline, thus adding fuel to their original anger.

Their mounting anger creates more adrenaline surges, resulting in more self-condemnation for being angry or in greater fear of loss of control, such as the fear of destroying property or lashing out at others. These heightened fears can produce even more adrenaline surges, and therefore more anger, and so forth.

Some rape survivors experience an additional level of guilt attached to feeling angry, which can further fuel this vicious cycle. On some level, perhaps unconsciously, they equate being angry with being a perpetrator. Even if their attacker did not make angry statements during the assault, his actions epitomized anger. Hence, their feelings of hostility, however meager, make them feel as if they have become perpetrators themselves. The resulting shame and guilt can lead to an unhealthy suppression of anger or to anger at being angry, which escalates the anger cycle.

The Numbing Cycle

The same spiral process can occur with numbing. As women become aware that they are beginning to dissociate, they may fear the dissociation will escalate to the point that they won't be able to function. But such fright, even if experienced only intellectually, usually speeds up the numbing process. This leads to more worries, resulting in more numbing symptoms, thus confirming the fear of becoming immobilized, possibly forever.

If your healing efforts stimulate one of these vicious cycles or other symptoms, you may be tempted to abandon your recovery work altogether. Working with the exercises in this book can help stop these vicious cycles before they start up, so that you can continue to heal.

Your Safety Plan

In the past, you may have tried to manage distress through substance abuse, an eating disorder, self-mutilation, or another self-harming behavior. As Bass and Davis (1988) put it, these may have been the only ways you found to emotionally stabilize yourself.

However, these can no longer be options for you. In this chapter you will create a constructive alternative to self-harm in the form of a safety plan for coping with anxiety, anger, numbing, and flashbacks or intrusive thoughts. How often you use your safety plan is not as important as the fact that you have one. Having a written plan at your fingertips, as well as a phone list of helpful people and places, can have a calming effect, even if you never use your plan or call a single person on your list.

Some techniques described here will work for you, some will not. It doesn't really matter which ones you select as long as they help you, even a little, and do not create more stress. *They all have the same goal: to introduce a moment of thought between feeling distressed and your reactions to that distress.* Your ability to call upon the powers of your mind when your emotions and body are in an uproar, however, is possible only if you can learn to view your symptoms realistically, in terms of what they really are: normal biological reactions to sexual assault.

Examining Your Thoughts

When you feel the first signs of anxiety, what are your immediate thoughts? Do you tell yourself, "I'm not going crazy. All I'm feeling is anxiety because I'm having a trigger reaction and my adrenal glands are pumping adrenaline into my system"? When you feel yourself beginning to go numb, do you think, "I don't need to be afraid of how I'm feeling. I must be on overload or be reacting to a reminder of the assault, and my body is trying to calm me down by releasing neurohormones that cause a numbing reaction"?

When you have a nightmare, intrusive thought, or flashback, do you view these as ways of helping you heal by releasing a little bit more of the assault? When you become angry, do you ever remind yourself that being able to feel anger is a sign of being emotionally alive? Do you ever stop and ask yourself, "Am I only angry, or am I also hurt, afraid, or sad?"

Most likely you tell yourself nothing of the kind. Instead your thoughts may be similar to this: "What's wrong with me that I am still reacting this way? No matter what I do, how much therapy I get, and how hard I try, I can't get better. I'll probably be like this until the day I die. Don't tell anyone. They'll think I'm crazy."

When you automatically interpret one of your symptoms as meaning that you are deficient or doomed for eternity to pay for another person's crime, the stress generated by such self-denigrating catastrophic ideas can increase the amount of adrenaline or noradrenaline in your body. As a result, without intending to do so, you may be diving into one of the vicious cycles described above, wherein your *reaction* to your reactions creates even more distress, leading to despair.

Your trigger reactions are not measures of your personal worth or character and, in themselves, they do not have the power to predict the future. If you cut your finger and it bled, you would not immediately conclude that bleeding meant you were a psychological wreck and that you'd never be happy again. However, in the popular mind, these biochemical reactions are assumed to be "mental" and therefore under individual control. As a result, you may view having these reactions as a lack of willpower or personal strength.

These views are false and you need to remind yourself repeatedly that they are false. Well over a hundred years of research and many hundreds of scientific studies have proven that they are false and not one study has proven that they are true (Shephard 2001; van der Kolk, McFarlane, and Weisaeth 1996). Part of your safety plan will include advising yourself that it makes as much sense to berate yourself for having trigger reactions as it does to scold your cut finger for bleeding. Yet, because the reactions you experience at the moment are so similar to the ones you had during the assault, it can feel as if the assault is happening all over again in the present.

At such times you need to ground yourself in your present reality. Look around you. Is there danger? Unless you are actually in another life-threatening situation, you will need to tell yourself, "I'm safe. That was then. This is now"; or, "I am not being assaulted right now, even though it feels as if I am."

Feelings are not facts. Just because you feel as you did during the assault does not mean you are being assaulted in the present. Just because you feel afraid does not automatically mean there is danger. Stopping your negative catastrophic thoughts and distinguishing the present from the past and the future are invaluable ways to regain emotional control. (See appendix B for helpful books on countering self-defeating thinking.)

Coping with Anxiety

Common warning signs of anxiety include milder forms of any of the symptoms of anxiety listed in the beginning of this chapter; loss of balance; irritability; suspiciousness; excessive worrying; panic over minor matters; compulsive behavior; impulses to indulge in alcohol, drugs, excess food, or shopping or gambling sprees; and impulses to cut, burn, starve, or otherwise mutilate yourself or to do *anything* to make the anxiety go away.

Under nontraumatic conditions, people do not accelerate from a state of relative peace to one of near panic in five minutes. Usually, physical warning signs come first, followed by emotional or mental signals that anxiety is mounting It is easier to manage anxiety if you can catch it in its early stages, before your mind starts racing or your body feels like it's going to explode.

Exercise: Your Warning Signs of Anxiety

On a new page in your journal entitled "My Warning Signs of Anxiety," list your warning signs of anxiety. If you think that you don't have any, think again. Find a comfortable chair, close your eyes, and visualize the last time that you felt anxious. What were your physical sensations? What were your emotions? What were your thoughts?

Now visualize yourself a few hours (or a day or two) before your last anxiety crisis (where you were, what you were doing, what was happening around you). Imagine you are watching a video of yourself, from your first moments of anxiety to the point where you felt as if you were jumping out of your skin. As you review the progression of events where your mild tension grew into near panic, do you remember having any particular thoughts, feelings, or physical sensations? In retrospect, might any of these have been warning signs of anxiety?

Time-Tested Ways to Calm Yourself

Writing, sharing with others, exercise, meditation, yoga, muscle relaxation, and controlled breathing have been used for centuries throughout the world to help achieve inner calm. Visualizing a safe place you can go to regardless of your circumstances or visualizing someone or something you love, such as a pet or your garden, can be soothing. Concentration camp survivors, for example, frequently reported that what kept them alive was thinking about their loved ones, even if those individuals were dead.

These methods can be used on an emergency basis. However, they are most effective when they are practiced daily, so that, over time, they result in an overall decrease of bodily tension that is demonstrated by a more normal blood pressure and heart rate. This decreased level of physical tension has many excellent effects, particularly in that it will take stronger or more frequent triggers to cause strong fight, flight, or freeze reactions.

As a result, you will have fewer trigger reactions. This, in turn, results in a stronger immune system and less stress on your body. Your emotional and mental stability also will improve, which can boost both your self-esteem and your functioning. This can begin a positive cycle where improved functioning leads to increased self-esteem, which enhances emotional and mental stability, leading to even more self-confidence and success, and so forth. As this positive cycle takes hold, the negative effects of the assault will diminish.

A note of caution: Before you begin any of the self-calming methods suggested in this book or in the resources listed in appendix B, obtain the approval of a physician, psychiatrist, or other mental health counselor. In some cases, the physiological changes induced by self-calming methods interact negatively with certain medical conditions or with certain psychiatric or nonpsychiatric medications. For some survivors, relaxation exercises bring forth intolerable memories. If this happens to you, stop immediately.

Also, these exercises may be detrimental if you were told to "relax" or breathe in certain ways during the assault, if you have a history of dissociating, if you dissociated during the assault, or if you have been told by a mental health professional that you dissociate frequently (even if you don't believe it). *If you fall into any of these categories, do not begin any self-calming exercises unless you have been given specific medical permission to do so.*

Quick Fixes

These quick fixes may seem superficial or simplistic, but they might get you through moments of mounting anxiety. You may need to experiment with a number of methods to determine which ones work for you. Use any combination of techniques that works for you. Place your right hand near the top of your left breast, rub your fingers gently in a circle, and say out loud at least three times, "Even though I am anxious (or have a certain problem), I deeply and completely accept and love myself." Watch five minutes of television or a video. Listen to music. Pick up a spoon and pretend it is holding hot tea, then blow on the spoon slowly, so as not to spill the tea. Complete a small chore, like folding laundry or vacuuming one room (one room only). Have a cup of tea or warm milk. Look at pictures of people or places that you love. Think about people, music, places, scents, foods, or any memories or other aspects of your life that give you comfort and hope. Tend to a pet. Do something for someone else or ask others what they do to help calm themselves.

Caution: Using these techniques only during emergencies will not permanently lower your level of body tension, and using them frantically can even increase your level of anxiety (Winston 2001). However, using them with an attitude of acceptance of your anxiety and of compassion toward yourself can be beneficial in a pinch.

Coping with Anger

Anger is a deep and complicated emotion. You may need more help than the coping skills listed below and those provided in chapter 10. Some of the techniques listed in "Quick Fixes" above might also be helpful. If you have suicidal, homicidal, or sadistic fantasies, or if you fear that you might lose control of your anger or if you have done so in the past (even once), seek additional help immediately. It is beyond the scope of this book to offer a complete anger-management program. Consult appendix B for additional help.

Immediate Anger-Management Techniques

The techniques listed here are not designed to eliminate the root causes of your anger. Yet they may be able to help you control your anger in the moment. Take a time-out from whatever you are doing: instead, play the piano, bang on a drum (use a cooking pot if you don't have a drum), stomp your feet, push against a wall, or do any form of physical exercise that doesn't harm you or others. Yell or scream (but not at anyone else or at a pet). Talk to someone safe about your anger. Or, if you believe in a higher power, tell that entity about your anger.

You can also make a list of all the things you are mad about or draw a picture of your anger (either of which you can discard later) or speak your anger into a tape recorder (you can later erase the tape). These expressions of anger probably will not eliminate your anger, but they can reduce it and help you to see it more clearly.

The instruction given here to discard your writings or drawings or to erase your recordings is not intended to imply that you should not be angry. Rather, disposing of these expressions of your anger can be a symbolic way to release your anger, as well as protecting you from the possibility that they might be found by someone not on your safe list. For example, a letter brimming with rage toward your attacker may disturb a child, or be cause for criticism by a relative or friend who feels threatened by your anger or who disapproves of women being angry.

Exercise: Your Warning Signs of Anger

Like anxiety, managing anger is much easier if you notice it before it turns from mild annoyance to rage. Relax for a few minutes, then think about the last few times you have become angry—not frustrated, but angry. Looking back, what were you thinking, feeling, and experiencing in your body before your irritation turned into full-blown anger? What were your warning signs of anger? What could you have done to help yourself at that time? On a new page in your journal called "My Warning Signs of Anger," list your warning signs of anger.

Coping with Numbing and Dissociation

In her book *The Truth about Rape*, author Teresa Lauer (2002) writes about times when she heard herself talking, yet felt as if she was hearing a different person. Her words were disconnected and lacked emotion. She had trouble concentrating and communicating what was truly in her heart. She was there, but not there.

Like Teresa, since your assault, you may have had times when you feel that you are not totally present in your life. Your mind feels sluggish; your emotions subdued. Your interest in people, work, and social activities wanes. As one survivor put it, "I turn into a vegetable, that is, no feelings." If a medical or substance abuse problem isn't causing the numbing, you may be dissociating as a defense against the unbearable emotions associated with your assault.

Numbing or dissociating is a form of blocking. The blocking can be partial or total and may be physical, mental, or emotional, or a combination of all three. Dissociation, commonly referred to as "shutting down," "spacing out," "zoning out," or "going fuzzy," describes not only the biological changes that occur during sexual assault, but also the wish that the assault wasn't happening. When women can't escape their assailants, they can flee mentally by dissociating. This helps them feel that the assault isn't real and helps them to preserve some of their identity and self-respect.

When Dissociation Is Severe

Everybody dissociates to one degree or another some of the time. To misplace your keys occasionally is quite normal. However, misplacing them every third or fourth time you use them is a sign of severe dissociation requiring professional care. Other forms of severe dissociation that require *prompt attention* include frequent sleepwalking or traveling away from home without remembering your name or how you got to your present location; "losing time," that is, suddenly noticing that some time has passed and you can't remember what occurred during that time; feeling no emotion for long periods of time; not experiencing physical pain or extreme heat or cold when it would normally be expected; and any form of dissociation that poses a potential danger to yourself or others.

Exercise: Your Warning Signs of Numbing

Like anxiety, going numb usually doesn't happen all at once. Typically, there are warning signs. The greater your awareness of your warning signs, the greater the probability that you can take charge of your dissociation. Close your eyes, relax for a few minutes and think about the last few times you found yourself going numb, physically, emotionally, or mentally. What was happening then or a few hours or days before? As you review these events, can you remember what you were thinking or feeling? Can you notice or remember any early signs of numbing? On a new page in your journal entitled "My Warning Signs of Numbing," make a list of the warning signs that indicate you are beginning to dissociate.

Ways to Ground Yourself

When you observe yourself beginning to dissociate, consider the following ways to ground yourself in the reality of the present. Disregard any suggestion that might remind you of the assault. For example, if body lotions or flowers played a role in your assault, do not use any grounding techniques that involve lotions or flowers. You may need to experiment with a number of methods to determine which ones work for you. Use any combination of techniques that work for you.

Physical grounding. Change your clothes; take a bath; touch a safe item (a chair, your clothing, hair, or shoes) or a familiar item you associate with comfort (a stuffed animal, a soft piece of cloth, pictures of people you love); exercise; do mindless chores; brush your teeth; apply hand or body lotion; drink water; move your hands or feet; focus your eyes on a safe item in the room; play loud music or ask whomever is with you to talk a little louder; walk around the room; brush your cat or dog; make contact with nature; play a musical instrument; or say your name out loud several times. (Keep safe and comforting items, such as stuffed animals or pieces of soft cloth, nearby in case you need them.)

Emotional grounding. Talk to someone, write, pray; look at yourself in a mirror and tell yourself how you feel (provided mirrors are not a trigger for you); write yourself a letter or an email and send it to yourself; leave a message on your phone for yourself, telling what you are experiencing at that very moment; make contact with nature; play a musical instrument; or make a list of five people you love and say, "I love you" out loud to each person on the list.

Mental grounding. Describe the room you are in, the colors, the furniture, the size (out loud or in writing); read out loud from a magazine or book; say the names of your relatives, friends, or favorite flowers or foods; sing; describe the weather; describe your plans for the rest of the day or the upcoming weekend; or say what day and time it is.

Caution: Do not drive (a car, truck, or plane); ride a bike or motorcycle; cook; stand on ladders; go rock or mountain climbing, swim, ski, or engage in any sport that requires focus, balance, or concentrated effort; babysit children; tend to pets; handle scissors, saws, or other tools or potentially dangerous items; handle glass or other fragile items, chemicals, or weapons; make any major decisions or commitments. Avoid any people, images, places, objects, or activities that remind you in any way, however small, of the sexual assault or of any other traumatic or stressful event.

Coping with Flashbacks and Intrusive Thoughts

Flashbacks. During flashbacks, you are suddenly transported back in time where you relive bits and pieces of the assault or the entire horror in full detail. Flashbacks are usually thought of as visual, in that you see all or portions of the assault as if it were happening in front of you. But there are also auditory flashbacks, where you hear sounds associated with the assault; olfactory flashbacks, where you smell odors associated with the assault; and somatic flashbacks, where your body reexperiences some or all of the pain or other bodily sensations related to the assault. For example, if your arm was broken during the attack, at various times afterward, it may ache as if it were still broken.

Perhaps the most disturbing aspect of a flashback is not the flashback itself, but the destabilizing feelings that come with it. Flashbacks are not just memories, but memories accompanied by strong emotions. Therefore, whether you have an auditory, visual, or other type of flashback, you are likely to experience the horror and other emotions associated with the assault.

There are also emotional flashbacks where you suddenly experience the emotions you had during the assault. Often these feelings seem to descend upon you out of nowhere. "Everything was okay, but then I just started shaking (or sweating, or crying, or getting mad) for no reason," survivors often say. But there are plenty of good reasons for these reactions, as described earlier in this chapter.

Intrusive thoughts. Unwanted thoughts about the assault, or any mistreatment you suffered afterward, are called "intrusive thoughts." Not only are they unbidden, but it feels like such a struggle, if not an impossibility, to get them out of your mind. Like flashbacks, intrusive thoughts are accompanied by shock, terror, and other reactions associated with the assault.

Unlike anxiety and numbing, flashbacks and intrusive thoughts have few warning signs. Although they tend to be more frequent and intense when you are triggered, for the most part, they are unpredictable. Nevertheless, there are ways you can manage these symptoms. The grounding skills for numbing outlined above also can be used to cope with flashbacks and intrusive thoughts. See appendix B for trauma-processing books that provide additional suggestions for managing these and other trigger reactions not covered in this book, such as insomnia, nightmares, depression, addiction, and phobias.

Exercise: Safety Plan

In this exercise, you will create a safety plan to help you manage anxiety, anger, numbing, flashbacks, and intrusive thoughts. Even if you have not experienced all of these trigger reactions, or you feel you are in control of all your triggers, you need to complete this exercise for all of the symptoms listed. Hopefully, you will never develop additional symptoms or never lose control over the ones you are managing successfully today. However, in case you do, you need to be prepared. In your journal, on a new page titled "My Safety Plan," copy the following format and answer all of the questions. You will need more than one page to complete this exercise.

1. Attitude Check: How Am I Feeling about Myself Right Now?

For anxiety: Am I judging my anxiety? Am I berating and shaming myself for being anxious, or can I accept that this feeling is normal for survivors? The rape survivor in me was frightened and humiliated by the assailant. Do I really want to scare her and beat her up, too, just like he did? I can write in my journal or talk to someone on my safe list to help me with my attitude.

For anger: Am I judging my anger? Can I accept my anger as a normal response to having been assaulted, or do I believe that being angry turns me into an undesirable horrible woman? I have the right to be angry about what happened to me, but I do not have the right to use my anger destructively. I can write in my journal or talk to someone on my safe list to help me with my attitude.

For numbing: Am I judging my numbing? Am I berating and shaming myself for shutting down, or can I accept that this is normal for survivors? The rape survivor in me dissociated to protect herself from terror and degradation. Do I really want to scare and disrespect her, too, just like my attacker did? I can write in my journal or talk to someone on my safe list to help me with my attitude.

For flashback and intrusive thoughts: Am I judging my flashbacks or intrusive thoughts? Am I berating and shaming myself for them? Can I accept that these are reactions are normal for rape survivors? These symptoms disrupt my thinking and emotional stability. Do I really want to further erode my mental and emotional stability by chastising myself for having these involuntary reactions? I can write in my journal or talk to someone on my safe list to help me with my attitude.

2. Reality Check: What Is Really Happening Right Now?

For anger: Am I thinking clearly? Am I thinking that being angry means I'll automatically react to it destructively? If I fear I can't control my anger, I commit to seeking out additional help in anger management. In the future I commit to seeking out ways to use my anger energy for good.

For anxiety, numbing, flashbacks, and intrusive thoughts: Am I thinking clearly? Am I mistakenly assuming that being anxious (or becoming numb or having flashbacks or intrusive thoughts) means that the assault is taking place right now? What is happening right now in my surroundings? What is the present danger? Is it life-threatening?

Am I assuming that having this symptom means that another assault, or a similar terrible event, is destined to happen to me in the near future? Where is the evidence that this will occur? What is the probability that it will occur? Can I remember that I can write in my journal or talk to someone on my safe list to help me figure out how much danger I am in right now or will be in, in the future?

3. My Action Plan: What Can I Do to Help Myself?

For anxiety: Can I wait for my anxiety to subside without doing anything? If not, or at such time when the anxiety becomes intolerable, I can do this: (list at least seven self-calming methods you have used successfully in the past, or you have read about in this or other books, or that were suggested by your therapists or others).

For anger: Can I wait for my anger to subside? If not, or at such point when it is no longer tolerable to do nothing, these are some ways I can subdue my anger: (list at least seven anger-management methods you have used successfully in the past, you have read about in this or other books, or that were suggested by your therapists or others).

For numbing: Can I tolerate waiting for my numbing to subside? If not, or at such point when it is no longer tolerable to do nothing, these are some ways I can ground myself: (list at least seven grounding methods you have used successfully in the past, you have read about in this or other books, or that were suggested by your therapists or others).

For flashbacks and intrusive thoughts: Can I tolerate waiting for my flashback or intrusive thought to end? If not, or at such point where it is no longer tolerable to do nothing, these are some ways I can help myself: (list at least seven grounding methods you have used successfully in the past, you have read about in this or other books, or that were suggested by your therapists or others).

Additional help for anxiety, anger, numbing, flashbacks, and intrusive thoughts: If I try all the suggestions I've listed above and I am still uncomfortably distressed, I may need to repeat my attitude and reality checks. If these coping techniques don't help me and I begin to fear that I might lose control or act destructively, I will seek help immediately by contacting these resources: (list three sources of help or more from the medical and mental health safety contract you created in chapter 2).

4. Self-Reward: What I Can Do to Reward Myself?

For anxiety, anger, numbing, flashbacks, and intrusive thoughts: Regardless of the results of my efforts, I need to applaud myself for trying to manage my trigger reactions constructively, rather than doing nothing or reacting to them in a destructive manner. I also need to celebrate any other positive actions I took, however small, by rewarding myself, for example, by sharing my progress with someone who will rejoice for me and with me. *Add any additional comments or suggestions that you want to remember in your time of need.*

Using Your Safety Plan

Make copies of your safety plan and keep it where it is both safe and readily accessible. Practice and become familiar with all the techniques on your list. There is no guarantee that a method that usually helps you will always do so. On particularly stressful days or in especially difficult situations, you may need to check your attitude and thinking patterns several times or repeat a specific technique (or several techniques) until you regain some emotional composure. Reviewing your safety plan before or after each journal-writing session and sharing it with trusted others can help you to incorporate your safety plan as a part of you.

One common complaint among survivors goes like this, "But I don't have time for all these safety plans and coping exercises. If I do all that, I'll accomplish nothing all day except manage my emotions." In my view, coping constructively with your symptoms is accomplishing a lot. If in the past you dealt with them by addictive behavior or self-harm, the fact that you are trying safer ways now shows how far you have grown in self-love and in self-control. That you are able to think before you react is a far cry from the past when you reacted to assault triggers automatically and impulsively.

Now you are able to consider your options and make a conscious choice about how to act. This is a major achievement for anyone, but especially for a victim of sexual assault. Later on, you will be able to use this hard-won invaluable power to think before you react in recovering from the negative thoughts and behaviors stemming from the assault.

Exercise: Obstacles

What would prevent you from using your phone list or your safety plan? What would stop you from practicing your coping skills? In your journal on new page entitled "Obstacles," write three or four sentences identifying possible obstacles. For each obstacle you list, write about what you can do to help yourself overcome it. Ask for suggestions from people on your safe list who are also committed to a recovery process. Undoubtedly, they have encountered hindrances in using some of the tools of recovery.

Acceptance

Accepting the reality of the assault and its aftermath doesn't mean resigning yourself to a life of mood swings. It doesn't mean standing by helplessly while your pain overpowers you, much as your assailant overpowered you. Rather, it means acknowledging on a gut level that the assault happened. Mentally, you know that you were assaulted. But at times, your oh-so-justifiable wish that it was a just a bad dream can be so powerful that, even as you write and talk about the assault, you do so as if the assault hadn't really happened or, if it did, that its effects were inconsequential.

If, on some level, you haven't fully accepted what happened, then your symptoms might be even more hateful to you. Not only do they disrupt your life, they also remind you of an ugly reality you were hoping to forget. If you require medication, acupuncture, or other medical care, you may resent your dependence upon these treatments and their financial and other costs. Accepting the fact of the assault and its scars is painful. It involves grieving for your losses. In the words of one survivor, "'Accept the scars,' they all say. But how I wish, oh how I wish, the scars would go away."

Managing your trigger reactions with an attitude of acceptance doesn't mean you won't have negative feelings about them or any negative sensations. With help and efforts on your part, however, the frequency and anguish of these reactions and their ability to disrupt your life can lessen considerably. A few may disappear entirely. Ironically, what diminishes the negative effects of these symptoms on your life is accepting, not fighting, them (Winston 2001).

Some survivors have found that if they allow themselves to fully experience their distress, without judging it or doing anything to make it go away, it sometimes lifts on its own (Winston 2001). Sitting with your agony until it subsides may or may not be an option for you. Remember, if riding your distress until it runs its course is intolerable for you, this doesn't mean you are a failure. Simply proceed to the next step of your safety plan.

Checking in: Return to the "Directions for Checking In" at the end of chapter 1 and answer all the questions to the best of your ability.

CHAPTER 5

Facts and Myths about Sexual Assault

Knowledge Is Power

Healing is difficult enough without the added burden of coping with misinformation about sexual assault, most of which denigrates survivors. The more you learn about sexual assault, the less painful and complicated your recovery will be. This chapter provides some basic facts about it. Other survivors also can be a source of information. Some have written books, articles, and poems about their recovery. There may be survivors among your friends and family members. If you decide it's safe, talking to other survivors or participating in a survivors group conducted by qualified leaders can be extremely beneficial (see appendix A). As always, monitor your reactions as described in the "Cautions" section in the introduction.

The Myths of Sexual Assault

Sexual assault is so frightening and can feel so stigmatizing that even women whose sexual experiences meet the legal definition of rape do not "name" or label these incidents as such. Many women are unfamiliar with the full range of behavior that is considered sexual assault. Their perception of what constitutes "real" rape is clouded by the numerous myths about sexual assault that permeate our culture (Crawford and Unger 2000).

Some of the most widespread rape myths include the following:

1. Due to the women's movement, sexual assault rates are dropping.

2. Women often lie about rape.

3. Only attractive women get raped.

4. Only bad girls are sexually assaulted.

5. All women enjoy a little rape now and then.

6. Date rape isn't really rape.

7. If you didn't resist, you must have wanted it.

8. Men sexually assault or try to sexually assault women for sexual release.

9. Lesbians are less likely to be sexually assaulted than heterosexual women.

All of the statements above are false (Lonsway and Fitzgerald 1994). Over twenty years of research has disproved each of these myths, although they still are widely believed in our society. Close your eyes and imagine a woman who has been sexually assaulted. Be honest. Do you see a promiscuous woman; a junkie; a vengeful spurned lover; an ignorant or emotionally disturbed woman; or a woman who drank too much, who stupidly forgot to lock her door, or foolishly went walking or jogging near a high-crime neighborhood or in a dark isolated area?

If one of the pejorative images popped into your mind, don't be ashamed. These blatantly insulting stereotypes of sexual assault victims as liars, fools, neurotics, or women of little character are so prevalent that you cannot help but be influenced by them. They evolved during the many centuries that women were considered to be the property of men.

In the not so distant past, for a woman to prove that she had not consented to sexual relations, she had to convince a court of law both of her good reputation and that she had been physically coerced. She also had to prove "utmost resistance," that is, that she resisted with all her strength throughout the entire attack or until she was exhausted. Marital rape, like wife beating, had few legal consequences

Today, the requirement of "utmost resistance" no longer exists and, under certain conditions, husbands can be prosecuted for marital rape. Currently, victim shield laws limit the degree to which a woman's prior sexual history can be introduced as evidence in court. Furthermore, colleges are now required to assist victims and institute disciplinary hearings for the accused offenders.

Nevertheless, centuries of blame-the-victim laws and attitudes die hard. Victims are still asked if they have any cuts or bruises, if they screamed, if they had prior social or sexual relations with the accused, or if they experienced sexual arousal during the assault, as if arousal was proof of consent. In truth, even though a woman's prior sexual history is no longer admissible in court, her character is still on trial.

The past few decades have seen notable progress in establishing sexual assault as a serious crime and in apprehending and successfully prosecuting offenders. However, these improvements are far from universal. It takes time for new laws to be codified and, when they are on the books, they are often not enforced. It takes even longer for public attitudes to change.

Although you may reject traditional teachings about sexual assault, a part of you may still blame yourself for the assault, especially if you knew your attacker. You may look back in horror at your experience and wonder whether your prior sexual behavior or your secret fantasies somehow lured your assailant to your side. You may be calling yourself "stupid" for not having seen the assault coming, and wondering whether you are as competent as you once thought you were.

If you find that somewhere, down deep in your soul, you harbor negative attitudes toward survivors, yourself included, do not be alarmed. It is very hard to erase cultural conditioning, especially when the people who matter to you—your family and friends—or people who have power over your life—court officials, police officers, and medical or mental health personnel—either directly or indirectly express indifferent or hostile attitudes toward you or other rape survivors. Their lack of empathy, at the time when you most need understanding, may confirm your belief that some inadequacy or defect within yourself brought about your assault.

Overcoming mistaken notions about sexual assault involves first, recognizing what they are, and then challenging the thinking and factual basis behind them. In this chapter, various myths about sexual assault are presented, then disconfirmed. Hopefully, after you finish reading this chapter, your image of a survivor will be that of a competent self-respecting woman who was unjustly violated by a man who used sex as a weapon.

Myth Number One: Sexual Assault Rates Are Dropping

Sexual assault has been called the fastest-rising violent crime in the United States (Wolf 1991). It is not clear, however, whether greater percentages of women are being attacked or whether these increased rates reflect a greater willingness of women to report this crime, along with improved reporting procedures. What is clear, however, is that sexual assault is not a rare occurrence, but a highly prevalent practice.

According to the Uniform Crime Reports, at least one woman is raped every six minutes in the United States (FBI Uniform Crime Reports 1991). Including all forms of sexual assault, an estimated 24 to 54 percent of American women are attacked in their lifetime, with anywhere from one-fourth to one-third experiencing assaults that meet or closely resemble legal definitions of forcible rape (Petrak and Hedge 2002). These figures do not include lesbian assaults, prison assaults, or other unreported rapes. Throughout the world, an estimated 20 percent of adult women are raped (using definitions of rape similar to U.S. legal standards).

In South Africa, a woman is raped every minute and a half (Petrak and Hedge 2002). During all the wars in recorded history, the rape of enemy women was, and still is, considered a "right" of the victor, part of the "spoils" of war. In the 1990s, mass rape became an official "strategy" during the wars in the Balkans and in Congo, Africa. Today there are government officials on trial in the World Court for promoting rape as a military strategy, a weapon of war.

Myth Number Two: Women Often Lie about Rape

Women have been accused of lying about rape from time immemorial, and some women do make false allegations of sexual assault, just as some make false allegations of physical battery. According to police statistics, approximately 8 percent of reports of forcible rape, as compared to 2 percent of reports for all crimes, are false or lack sufficient supporting evidence. Feminists argue that this 8-percent figure has more to do with the tendency of law enforcement officers to view certain types of assaults as not being "real" rape, for example, assaults by acquaintances or former lovers, assaults occurring in the victim's or the offender's residence, and assaults by men who have no criminal record or psychiatric diagnosis (Hall 1995).

Even if 8 percent of women do lie about rape, they are the exception, not the rule. If there is any rule, it is that sexual assault is by far the most underreported crime in the United States (National Crime Victim Center 1992). Although the FBI estimates that only 10 percent of completed rapes are not reported, police data and the results of a national survey of sexual assault centers indicate that 50 percent are not reported (Hall 1995).

However, many experts feel that this 50-percent figure grossly underestimates the degree of underreporting. Underreporting is especially prevalent among illegal and recent immigrants, among women from cultural groups that value sexual chastity, and among women who were attacked by someone they knew (Petrak and Hedge 2002).

Minority Women

The limited information we have indicates that African-American and Hispanic-American survivors, as compared to European-American survivors, face more negative social reaction if they disclose attempted or completed rape (Crawford and Unger 2000). Of all groups in the United States, Hispanic women have been found to have the highest rates for staying silent and the lowest rates of asking for help from others. Sexual assault is considered such a stigma that, clearly, many suffer in silence rather than risk social disapproval and rejection (Ullman and Filipas 2001). Except for some personal accounts, research on Native-American women is almost nonexistent.

The Effects of Backlash

The anti-rape movement of the 1970s resulted in greater public awareness of sexual assault and improved recording procedures and legislation, making it easier for women to come forward. However, within less than two decades, this progress was and continues to be undermined by a backlash that dismisses sexual assault as "rape hype" and feminist propaganda. This movement also alleges that researchers exaggerate statistics. (Media Education Foundation 1992) and that date-rape victims "cry rape" as an excuse for "bad sex" or, like Potiphar's wife, for vindictive or other illegitimate reasons (Roiphe 1993).

Women who recalled repressed memories of childhood sexual abuse were and are accused of lying to gain attention or financial compensation or of waging a personal vendetta against a family member for reasons unrelated to any sexual abuse. Therapists are being criticized for planting "false memories" of abuse in unsuspecting clients. There have even been efforts to eliminate federal funding for rape crisis centers (Gilbert 1993).

These and other forms of backlash have silenced and continue to silence women who have been sexually attacked, causing some women to wish that they had been mutilated as well as raped, so that they would be believed and respected as truth-tellers, and not viewed as liars.

Myth Number Three: Only Attractive Women Get Raped

Do you blame your assault on your looks? Think again. When an attractive woman is sexually assaulted, the attack is blamed on her looks. However, when a woman who hardly fits the cultural stereotype for attractiveness, such as a disabled, obese, or elderly woman, is victimized, she is viewed as having provoked or fabricated the assault to get attention or to be seen as sexually desirable (Hall 1995). Since women of all body types and all ages are sexually assaulted, looks can not be considered a cause of rape.

Being attractive is not an invitation to sexual assault. In our society, women are expected to make themselves appealing to men. In some circles, women are even pressured to dress provocatively and praised when they do. Yet even blatantly seductive clothing is not an excuse for sexual assault. As a rule, a woman's vulnerability and availability have more to do with her being selected as victim than her appearance.

Myth Number Four:
Only Bad Girls Get Sexually Assaulted

Were you ever told that good girls don't get assaulted, only bad girls? Were you taught that the only women who are attacked are those who overtly, subtly, or unconsciously "asked for it?" Were you raised to believe that it's the woman's responsibility to put limits on a man's sexual advances and, if she couldn't, she was probably promiscuous? Such attitudes betray a double standard of sexuality. According to this double standard, sexual feelings and expression are acceptable for men, but not for women, "good women," that is. Although this double standard is not as widespread as it used to be, it has not vanished. According to surveys, two-thirds of Americans believe that women provoke rape by their appearance or behavior, and that women engage in sexual contact voluntarily, then cry assault later (Allegeier and Allegeier 1991).

Myth Number Five: All Women
Enjoy a Little Rape Now and Then

Does a part of you believe this myth, too, even in part? Don't be ashamed if your answer is yes. It's almost impossible to escape the daily bombardment of pornographic or semipornographic images of women in the media. Women who enjoy sexual victimization, or give the appearance of enjoying it, are also glorified in popular songs and movies, and described in detail in novels, short stories, and even psychology and psychiatry books. Such thinking is fallacious. As Russell (1975) explains, women's rape fantasies have more to do with their sexual oppression than with any desire to be violated. If there was no sexual double standard, women would not need to view assault as a means of obtaining sexual gratification. Like men, they could enjoy their sexuality free of guilt, as often as they wished.

Certainly, today's women are not shackled by the sexual taboos of the past. Yet there is ample evidence that the double standard still is operative, although perhaps in more subtle forms. Significant numbers of middle school, high school, and college students of both sexes express more disrespect for sexually active unmarried women than for unmarried males who engage in exactly the same sexual behavior (Crawford and Unger 2000).

Furthermore, preliminary research indicates that up to one-third of college men who endorse equal sexual rights for women also report that they wouldn't consider marrying a woman with a history of many lovers (Crawford and Unger 2000). In sum, it is permissible, if not expected, for a woman to make herself as alluring as possible. However, if she acts on her sexual desires, she is still more likely to be considered immoral than a man who does the same.

If you doubt this last statement, complete the following journal assignment.

Exercise: The Double Standards of Sexual Behavior

On a new page in your journal entitled "The Double Standards of Sexual Behavior," draw a line down the middle of the page. On the left-hand side write all the nouns and adjectives you have heard to describe sexually active unmarried women, including adolescent girls. On the right-hand side, do the same for sexually active unmarried males. Include any slang words you heard while growing up or any you hear today in conversation or in the media. You do not have to believe these labels are true or fair, only that you have heard them used.

Compare your two lists. Probably negative and positive sounding words are on both. Overall, however, which sounds more positive, the male or the female list?

Usually, the male list sounds more positive. For example, sexually active men are commonly called "players," "studs," or "Romeos"; sexually active women, "sluts," "whores," and worse. Being a "player" implies insincerity, but it also implies having enough intelligence, verbal ability, and sex appeal to charm a woman into bed. In contrast, being a "slut" requires no special abilities except participation in casual sex. In some cultural and religious traditions, extramarital sex is forbidden for both sexes. Yet women who break the rules are punished more harshly than men who do so. For example, in the "honor killings" of certain Islamic societies, the woman who has had forbidden sex is killed by a family member to salvage the family's honor. Her partner may be chastised, but he is not killed.

As a result of this worldwide double standard, women learn that having sexual desires is bad and degrading. Having fantasies about sexual assault, however, permits a woman to enjoy her sexual self without having to take responsibility for her sexual desires. As Russell (1975) stresses, having fantasies of being raped and actually being attacked are not the same. When you fantasize about rape, you are in control. In real-life rape, you are not in control. On the contrary, you are subject to physical injury, even death.

"But in *my* rape fantasies I am beaten and hurt," you might be thinking. Don't be alarmed. Other women have such thoughts as well. If your fantasies include some pain, this does not mean you are neurotic or that you asked for the assault or any brutalization that may have accompanied it. The element of pain in your fantasies may simply be a way of punishing yourself for having sexual desires.

Think about it. Compare your actual assault to your fantasy assault. During the real-life assault, wasn't your dominant reaction fear rather than sexual pleasure? What about the many ways your attacker might have used to humiliate and terrorize you? If you really enjoyed the assault, why would you be in so much pain today?

There are some current theories that speculate some women are chemically, genetically, or emotionally "attracted" or "addicted" to violence. Such ideas are as stupid and unfounded as the centuries-old notion that women secretly enjoy sexual victimization. All these theories blame the victim and assume women can control male behavior.

Myth Number Six:
Date Rape Isn't Really Rape

Were you assaulted by a someone you knew? Even if it was your husband, boyfriend, date, or friend who forced himself on you, his violation of your body is just as much of a sexual assault as if he were a total stranger. Acquaintance or date rape is real and can hurt as much, if not more, than being assaulted by a stranger. Research has found that women assaulted by strangers tend to experience more fear and remain fearful for a longer period of time. Women assaulted by an acquaintance or date tend to suffer from more self-doubt (Crawford and Unger 2000).

If you were a victim of acquaintance rape, your trust in men may have taken an even greater blow than if you had been attacked by a stranger. You were betrayed and deceived, not by an unknown assailant, but by someone you loved, liked, or at least trusted enough to associate with socially. Also, you probably had more trouble being believed than do women assaulted by strangers, especially if you were or had been sexually or romantically involved with your attacker.

The Three Stages of Date Rape

Basically there are three kinds of date or acquaintance rape: beginning rape, early date rape, and relational date rape. Beginning date rape occurs on the first date. Often the man "is not a crazed psychopath, although he may display psychopathy-related traits" (Crawford and Unger 2002, 498). He may have made the date specifically to assault the woman. In early date rape, the assault occurs after a few dates. Typically, the victim wants to be "just friends," but the man wants to sexualize the relationship and forces the woman. In relational date rape, the couple has already engaged in kissing and light sexual activity, but not intercourse. The man may feel that intercourse is his due because of the money he has spent or because he thinks it is necessary to prove that the relationship is "going somewhere" (Wade and Cirese 1991).

If the woman and the man have had sexual contact prior to the assault it is still a crime if, on a particular occasion, the woman does not want sexual contact and the man forces himself upon her physically. It is also a crime if he coerces her into sexual activity using psychological manipulations, such as threatening to end the relationship, or using his greater power to harm her. For example, at work, he could threaten to promote or fire her; in school, he could give her a passing or failing grade; as her landlord, he could forgive her debt or evict her. Just because a woman has willingly had sexual contact with a man previously does not mean he has the right to coerce her into any form of sexual activity at another time.

Myth Number Seven: If You Didn't Resist, You Must Have Wanted It

Did you resist the assault, or did you submit? If you resisted, are you chastising yourself for not resisting "enough"? If you didn't put up a fight, are you calling yourself a "coward" or a "wimp"? On the basis of this single event, have you jumped to the false conclusion you are so ineffective that you'll never amount to anything in life? If so, it's important to realize that your going limp was the result of noradrenaline reactions (as described in chapter 4) and sex-role conditioning.

The obstacles that inhibit women from fighting back are not only physical. Psychological obstacles can be equally, or even more, powerful. Unless you somehow miraculously escaped the influence of sexism in your life, you were undoubtedly exposed to the idea that women aren't supposed to compete with men, or even to show anger toward them. From early childhood on, most girls are taught to please and obey, not to display or experience physical strength, assertiveness, and independence.

If you went limp during the assault, you were only reacting the way you were trained to react. You may also have hoped to avoid injury by being submissive. Perhaps you were explicitly warned that you'd be punished if you struggled, or instinctively sensed that resisting would either precipitate or escalate the use of physical force.

There is no conclusive evidence as to whether it is better to fight back or to submit, probably because each assault is unique. Some women who fought back, pleaded with the attacker, or offered him money have managed to escape or dissuade him. Other women who tried the same approaches found that fighting back or pleading only instigated even more savage beating. On the other hand, some women who submitted without a fight believe that their surrender saved their lives. Still others found that their passivity angered their attacker. "He wanted a woman with 'spunk,'" one woman reported. "He beat me because I was 'no fun.'"

Police officers and others who work with the problems of sexual assault on a daily basis cannot say with any authority what is the best way to stop an offender. If people with considerable professional experience in dealing with sexual assault do not know the "right thing to do," why should you, for whom the assault was a total shock, have known instantaneously what the best course of action would have been? Perhaps you can take comfort in research that shows that there are no personality differences found between women who resisted, women who didn't resist, and women who had never been sexually assaulted (Crawford and Unger 2002).

The recent trend in films portraying women martial artists and self-defense experts is sometimes used to support the idea that "no woman can be raped against her will." In my clinical work, however, I have found that even women with military, police, and other forms of intense self-defense training have been forced to submit to their attacker's instructions. Even some of these women "froze."

Sexual Pleasure and Orgasm during an Assault

You may have felt that your body betrayed you in ways other than not being able to fight back. Did you lubricate during the assault, experience sexual arousal, or have an orgasm? Were you shocked to find your body responding in such a manner? Are you now ashamed to admit your level of arousal?

You may not have been sexually aroused at all (which is not a reflection of your sexuality). However, if you were, you need to know that a sexual response during rape is not uncommon. If you did respond sexually, you may feel deeply guilty, as if your physical self's response somehow indicates that you "liked it" or "you asked for it." Before you chastise yourself for one more minute, remember that your sexual organs do not have a brain. They cannot distinguish between a mauling rapist and the gentle touch of a lover. They simply react to stimulation the way they were physically designed to respond.

Sexual arousal does not mean consent. If you climaxed or had some other sexual response to the assault, this does not mean you enjoyed it. Even women who climax several times during an assault say, "Yes, I came, but I hated it." If the rapist insisted on stimulating you or demanded a sexual response from you, you had little choice in the matter. Suppose your attacker did not deliberately stimulate you and did not demand you to display signs of arousal, such as flushed cheeks, lubrication, or orgasm, but you responded sexually anyway. This may have occurred simply because you are sexually alive. Sexual aliveness is a positive quality, not a curse.

Placating the Offender

After the assault, did you agree to see the offender again? Did you cook dinner for him, mend his clothing, spend time with him, or in other ways act as if he were your friend or caring lover, not your assailant? Are you ashamed to admit to such behavior?

If so, perhaps your shame and self-doubt can be reduced by appreciating the fact that when the offender overcame you physically, he also crushed your spirit and sense of autonomy. Your behavior following the assault was simply an extension of his crime, not an expression of something inherently wrong with you. It may be that you had a very powerful reason to be friendly and placate him, that is, to avoid physical harm not only to yourself but to your children or other loved ones.

Myth Number Eight: Men Sexually Assault or Try to Sexually Assault Women for Sexual Release

Sexual assault involves sexual behavior and sex organs; yet it is not a sexual act and has very little to do with sexual passion. Sexual assault is a violent act in which sex is used as a weapon. For this reason, sexual assault has been called a "pseudosexual act," because in the majority of cases it is committed to satisfy nonsexual needs.

For example, research has shown that very few rapists are lonely, socially inadequate men who rape because they lack a sexual partner. Most rapists have at least one sexual partner, if not more (Hall 1995). The typical offender is self-centered, has hostile and domineering attitudes toward women, and has a history of family violence, sexual promiscuity, and alcoholism (Crawford and Unger 2000).

However, offenders also can be "ordinary" guys. Surveys of college men indicate that one-third of those surveyed said that they could see themselves coercing a woman into having sex with them if they knew they would not be caught (Media Education Foundation 1992). These men are products of a society where sexual violence is frequently condoned. They are also influenced by popular beliefs such as these: women pretend and say "no" when they mean "yes;" or a man has the right to force sex on a woman if she agreed to have sex and then changed her mind, if she was disrobed, if he had touched her genitals or she had touched his, if he had spent a lot of money on her, or if they were dating exclusively. Such beliefs are still held by many women, as well as by many men (Hall 1995).

Power, Anger, and Sadism

Sexual assaults can be divided into three categories: power rape, anger rape, and sadistic rape (Groth, Burgess, and Holmstron 1977). Studies of convicted offenders indicate that most sexual assaults, especially gang rapes, are premeditated. This does not mean that specific women are targeted for assault. These findings should help to relieve you of any fears you might have that it was something you did or something about you that caused your assault.

Power rape. Men who feel powerless or frustrated in life may assault women to make themselves feel more powerful. Financial problems can put men into positions of relative powerlessness. When they cannot find a job no matter how hard they search, they may resort to the most primitive and most available way of proving their power: abusing women and children. Because women and children are smaller and weaker, they are perceived as easy targets.

Anger rape. Men who are angry for any reason may act out their anger by assaulting women. Included in this group are men who are specifically angry at women due to a negative personal experience with a particular woman. For example, men who were sexually abused by a female relative have been found to be more likely to attack women than men who were not so abused (Condy et al. 1987).

Sadistic rape. In sadistic rape, the goal is to humiliate and hurt. Sadistic rape can include mental and physical abuse, the use of objects to penetrate the vagina and the anus, and many forms of nonsexual torture.

Myth Number Nine: Lesbians Are Less Likely to Be Sexually Assaulted Than Heterosexual Women

The rates of sexual assault of lesbian women are higher than those for heterosexual women (Duncan 1990). Perhaps this is the case because sexual assaults on lesbians are often hate crimes. They are attacks against not only the woman but her sexual preference.

When a lesbian reports an assault or seeks help, she frequently faces negative stereotypes of lesbians as promiscuous and antisocial. If she was assaulted by a man, the attack may be seen as "coming to her" (as a punishment for being a lesbian) or as a "way to make her right" (i.e., heterosexual). If a lesbian is assaulted by another woman, the assault may not be taken seriously, even if her injuries are serious. The same difficulties that lesbian women encounter also beset women who are bisexual or transgendered.

Exercise: Are the Myths about Sexual Assault Truly Myths or Are They True?

This chapter has presented evidence refuting some of the most widely held myths about sexual assault. However, you may still believe that these myths are facts and not myths. If so, you need to discuss these issues with a sexual assault counselor or a mental health professional or consult some of the resources in appendix B.

Checking in: Return to the "Directions for Checking In" at the end of chapter 1 and answer all the questions to the best of your ability.

CHAPTER 6

The Stages of Sexual Assault

Typically, assault survivors go through four stages: the anticipatory stage, the impact stage, the reconstitution stage, and the resolution stage (Hall 1995; Koss and Harvey 1991). Some survivors also have profound spiritual experiences. Your experience may not have been similar to those described here. This should not be a cause of concern. There are no "normal" assaults. Each assault is unique. However you experienced these stages, and whatever the impact the assault had on your emotions, physical health, sexuality, and relationships, your experience was true for you.

Stage I: The Anticipatory Stage

During the anticipatory stage, a woman may begin to sense that she is in danger. If she is attacked without warning, this stage may last but a split second. When there is time between the first hint of danger and the actual assault, however, at first she may not realize the full extent of the threat to her safety.

You may have thought, "I'm being paranoid. He's my boy-friend (husband, relative, friend of the family, friend of a friend, a rabbi or a minister, a teacher, someone who has never been attracted to me, someone who is supposed to be sexually safe). It's ridiculous to think he'd harm me." Also, you may have disregarded warning signs.

As the possibility of danger became increasingly clear, however, you may have tried to ward off the attack by plotting an escape, trying to reason with your assailant, or staying calm so as not to incite him to further violence. You may have prayed, tried to memorize every detail of the event, and even tried to remember anything you ever read or heard about sexual assault. Any prior violent situations you may have experienced might have flashed before your eyes.

During this anticipatory stage, some women dissociate or "space out." (See chapter 4 for more information on dissociation.) Dissociation can be mental, emotional, physical, or a combination of these. If you dissociated mentally, you may have felt as if you were enclosed in a black cloud: You couldn't think clearly, your memory was impaired, and you were only partially aware of your surroundings. If you dissociated emotionally, you felt few emotions. If you dissociated physically, you may have felt fatigued or had difficulty moving or talking.

It bears repeating that dissociation is a normal response to fear. Also, your awareness of danger may have been muted if you were never taught how to spot or avoid dangerous situations or people; if you were severely ill, mentally impaired, or under the influence of drugs or alcohol; or if you were in shock due to another major loss, for example, if you were assaulted soon after a death in your family. If you were given a "date rape" drug such as Rohypnol (flunitrazepam) or gamma hydroxybutyrate (GHB), or another type of sedative, you may have had no, or barely any, awareness of the threat to your safety.

Stage II: The Impact Stage

The impact stage includes the actual assault and about two weeks following the assault. During the anticipatory stage, the woman still has hope. Despite her growing awareness of danger, at least a part of her still believes she can avoid an attack. During the impact stage when the assault actually occurs, any hope she had for an escape shatters. Unless she is already dissociated, the fear of death and feelings of helplessness and hopelessness fill every cell of her body.

The terror and horror can be so overwhelming you may have gone into disbelief, various degrees of physical and emotional numbness, or shock. Numbing can occur even if you never dissociated previously. If you began shutting down during the anticipatory stage, during the impact stage you may have shut down even more. You may have wondered, "Is this a dream? Can this really be happening to me?" or " I know it's happening to me, but why does it feel like it's happening to someone else?"

Some survivors have tried to remove themselves from the situation by thinking about irrelevant matters, such as whether the assault would make them late to their next appointment. Sometimes, survivors have out-of-body experiences where they feel they are observing the assault happening from a distance. For example, they may feel they are floating in the air near the ceiling or standing several feet away from the assault.

Immediately after the assault and for days afterwards, you may have stayed in a state of shock and disbelief. Like many survivors, at this point you may have begun to review what happened, berating yourself for being naive, for not having noticed the danger and taken action sooner, for not having escaped, for having shut down (or for showing your emotions), or for resisting (or not resisting). If there was little or no physical force involved but, instead, you were psychologically pressured by threats or by seductive professions of love, you may feel that you brought the attack upon yourself.

Resisting or Not Resisting

If you resisted, you may scold yourself for being so foolish as to have put yourself (or others, or a pet) at greater risk by not being clever, agile, or physically strong enough to have stopped the assault. If you didn't resist, you may see yourself as a coward or find yourself agreeing with Myth Number Seven (see chapter 5), that if a woman doesn't resist (enough), she must have "wanted it." Either way, shame and guilt usually follow.

Both resisting and not resisting are normal responses. Women who start out fighting back usually stop when they (or others) are threatened with serious harm if they do not "cooperate." They also stop when they see that their resistance entertains or sexually arouses the offender, or makes him more physically aggressive. Sexual assault is such an ever-present threat that some women plan what they will do if they are ever accosted.

Yet a woman doesn't always react as she had planned. "I decided long ago that I'd be passive. That way, maybe he wouldn't hurt me so much," said Annette. "Yet when it happened, I started hitting and biting him like a wild woman. I couldn't believe it was really me." In contrast, Joyce had an unexpected numbing reaction. "After my cousin was raped, I read every self-defense book I could get my hands on. But when I was jumped, I froze. I couldn't scream and I lost track of time. Even though I was burned with cigarette butts, I felt little pain. It was as if a thick blanket was covering my skin. I still wonder if he somehow drugged me."

If during the impact stage you dissociated, simply gave in, or did not resist to your satisfaction, this does not mean that you are cowardly, stupid, emotionally weak, or that you lack self-respect. Nothing could be further from the truth. The way people respond to situations of great danger depends more on certain involuntary physiological reactions to life-threatening circumstances, than on their personality, intelligence, or moral character. (See chapter 4 for an explanation of these physiological reactions.)

Controlled versus Emotional Reactions

During the impact stage, survivors lose their sense of safety, their faith in their judgment, and their faith in their ability to protect themselves. Immediately afterward, some survivors are flooded with shame, guilt, and other difficult emotions described below. For others, these emotional reactions emerge months, or even years, later. There is no "right or wrong" time to experience the effects of an assault, just as there is no "right or wrong" way to react to it. However and whenever the assault affected you is normal and right for you. Some survivors remain calm and controlled. Both reactions, the controlled and the emotional, are entirely normal.

Controlled Reactions

A woman may have a controlled reaction because of her enormous effort to be like a sturdy oak that can weather any storm rather than be a helpless victim, or because she is coping with other life crises that feel more urgent. Her inner psyche, in its wisdom, intuitively knows that spending psychic energy on self-condemnation would significantly detract from her ability to function.

A woman may also disown or repress any reactions to the assault that make her feel badly about herself, because at this crucial time, immediately after the assault, she desperately needs to affirm that, even though the attacker robbed her of her sense of safety, she still has her self-esteem and her emotional control. (When a woman *represses* a reaction, it is totally out of her awareness. When she *disowns* it, she views it as not belonging to her and pushes it aside whenever it enters her consciousness.)

A woman also may distance herself from any shame, guilt, or other negative feelings because she feels ashamed of being ashamed, and guilty about being guilty. In our culture, self-confidence and emotional self-control are highly valued. In many circles, shame, guilt, and other strong emotions are often viewed as psychological deficiencies and are therefore socially undesirable. Therefore, a woman may hide or suppress her feelings, especially her self-doubts, for fear others might view her as "hysterical," "weak," "overly emotional," or as "sitting on the pity pot."

Still other women disown their self-doubt and shame because having such feelings doesn't fit their view of themselves as competent and assertive or their history of professional or other successes, especially if they believe in women's rights. "I tell women all the time it isn't their fault," says Cora, a sexual assault counselor. "But after I was gang-raped, I started feeling almost as bad as they do. I simply cannot be feeling like this. I won't have it!" she declared, thus disowning this part of herself.

Emotional Reactions

If you had or are having some of the emotional reactions listed in the next paragraph, most likely they manifest themselves in troublesome ways. These emotions, born of trauma, can be powerful and intense, at least, initially. Therefore, they have a double impact: Not only are these feelings painful and disruptive in themselves, they can also make you feel as though the assault is happening all over again. Just as the attack was sudden, these emotions can arrive without warning. Just as you could not protect your body from being invaded by the attacker, you may now feel you can't protect yourself from being invaded by anxiety, depression, fear, shame, or other reactions.

Emotional reactions to sexual assault include fears of future sexual attacks on oneself or others, of going out alone, of sleeping alone, of unfamiliar places, and of others coming up behind you; feeling overwhelmed and unable to cope due to changes in relationships or lifestyle and also due to intrusive thoughts, mood swings, and other symptoms; grief; loss of innocence and loss of faith in a just world; helplessness and hopelessness; guilt and self-condemnation due to the belief that you should have thought, felt, or acted differently; shame or feeling your entire self is unacceptable or deficient (and is doomed to always be so); low self-esteem as manifested in feeling like "damaged goods," "a fallen woman," "a bad girl," "dirty," "defiled" or "ruined," or otherwise contaminated and inadequate; anger at yourself, the assailant, and others; and feeling dehumanized as if you were an object, not a person.

Somatic or Physical Problems

Quite commonly, survivors develop physical or somatic problems. If you had or are having some of the somatic reactions listed in the next section, it is likely that they, too, manifest themselves in troublesome ways. If you had a medical problem or a psychiatric illness before the assault, the assault may have made it worse. Usually, physical injuries sustained during an attack are taken seriously. However, some survivors have found that other normal somatic aftereffects, such as headaches and nausea, are dismissed as "psychological" or as childish pleas for unwarranted sympathy.

If this was your experience, you may wonder whether what others tell you is true, that your physical problems aren't real and you are just "being hysterical," or "overreacting," or "wallowing in self-pity." On the other hand, you know your discomforts are real. Even if your doctor gave you a clean bill of health, you may be concerned that your symptoms might be the first signs of potentially serious medical problems that the doctors failed to detect, or that reveal themselves only after some time has passed.

Yet you may avoid seeking help for fear that your symptoms will be dismissed as being "all in your head." If this is the case, you carry the burden of the anxiety about your health all alone, without the benefit of expert opinion. Your unanswered questions may create more anxiety, which often can exacerbate medical problems. If you find yourself in this situation, you are encouraged to review chapter 2 and to seek proper medical care, until you find a doctor who gives you the help you need.

Somatic or Physical Aftereffects of Sexual Assault

Sexual assault can lead to a number of physical or somatic symptoms. It can create concerns about one's health and aggravate any existing medical conditions. Common somatic aftereffects of sexual assault include sexually transmitted diseases; pregnancy; fatigue; headaches; backaches; stomach pains; general body pain; nausea; rectal pain and bleeding; urinary tract infections; uterine pain; urinary burning; skin problems; severe PMS; irregular menstrual cycles; and vaginal infections, itching, discharge, and pain.

Spiritual Experiences

It is not uncommon for women to have near-death, out-of-body, or other types of spiritual experiences during the assault, and to think seriously about religious and spiritual matters afterward. Others who come close to death, for example, on the operating table, in a automobile accident, or in a war zone, report similar experiences. Although your spiritual experiences may have brought you hope during the assault, you may now be keeping them a secret because they challenge your former religious or spiritual beliefs or those of your family, or because you fear others will think you are crazy.

You may also wonder whether your visions, out-of-body experiences, or other such reactions during the assault were truly spiritual experiences or instances of severe dissociation. One important difference is that dissociation involves feeling detached, not only from one's emotions and body (sometimes to the point of feeling dead or like a robot), but also from other people.

In contrast, spiritual experiences are described as feeling very alive and connected to a loving presence and to other people. If you are troubled by any of the concerns described here, you are encouraged to discuss them with a mental health professional or with a member of the clergy or spiritual leader of your faith.

The Biological Effects of Sexual Assault

Like the rest of the body, your central nervous system (CNS) is vulnerable. Given enough physical or emotional stress, it too can bend, or even break. When you were sexually assaulted, your CNS received a series of shocks. The greater the intensity and the longer the duration of the assault, and the greater the number of assaults, the greater the possibility that the delicate biochemical balances of your body might have been disrupted.

To date, there is no single definitive theory as to how traumas such as sexual assault affect the body. One theory holds that sexual assault destabilizes the autonomic nervous system; another posits that assault changes body chemistry so that the survivor becomes more prone to anxiety. Still another hypothesis holds that prolonged trauma depletes certain important neurotransmitters, which can result in mood swings, explosive outbursts, overreactions to subsequent stress, clinical depression, and symptoms of post-traumatic stress disorder. These depletions can result in overdependence on others, a helpless feeling like "I can't make it without you"—or its opposite—an unrealistically independent stance of "I don't need anyone; I can make it on my own."

However, these biochemical shifts are not experienced by every survivor. If you are a one-time survivor, these biological changes may not apply at all, or they may apply only under very limited circumstances, or for only a short period of time. Although all assaults potentially can have damaging physical effects, to date, research has examined only the biological effects of repeated sexual abuse or assaults that involved physical assault, as well. But there are no hard-and-fast rules about the biological consequences of trauma. For example, a woman who is raped, but not beaten, may suffer from biological changes as readily and as intensely as a survivor who received ten knife wounds.

Depression and Post-Traumatic Stress Disorder

Clinical depression and post-traumatic stress disorder are very common among survivors. For them, sleep becomes a nightmare of fear, restlessness, flashbacks, and terrifying dreams where one wakes up just at the point where one is going to die. A good night's sleep becomes an impossible dream. Depression, PTSD, and substance abuse are more prevalent among women who were violated as children or who, as adults, experienced multiple sexual assaults.

Depression

The major symptoms of depression include hopelessness, fatigue, depressed mood; sleeping and eating problems; social withdrawal; memory and concentration problems; inability to experience pleasure; and thoughts of death or suicide. About one-third of survivors develop a major depression after being attacked. This is three times the rate of depression among women who have not been victimized. One in every four or five survivors will actively consider suicide at some point after the attack. Studies have shown that many women experience relief from severe depression after three months; however, eight to ten years post-rape survivors, as a group, still evidenced higher rates of depression than women who had never been raped (Department of Veterans Affairs 1993).

Post-Traumatic Stress Disorder

Symptoms of Post-traumatic Stress Disorder (PTSD) include reliving symptoms such as flashbacks and intrusive thoughts; sleep disturbances, nightmares, and night terrors; hypervigilance or being constantly on the lookout for danger, and the startle response or jumpiness; numbing symptoms, such as avoiding thinking or talking about the assault or of reminders of the assault; feelings of doom involving fears of future assaults, illness, and other catastrophes, for yourself or loved ones; and mood swings and fears of mental instability, and even insanity.

PTSD rates for rape are higher than PTSD rates for any other crime. Some 90 percent of rape victims have been found to have PTSD symptoms the first month after the assault; about 50 percent, after three months; and a substantial percentage, for many months after the assault. Approximately 20 percent of survivors have been found to exhibit PTSD symptoms after seventeen years (Department of Veterans Affairs 1993).

Higher rates of PTSD have been found among survivors who blamed themselves for the assault, who sustained physical injuries, who decided to testify in court, who were assaulted in a safe location, who were raped in a nontraditional or deviant manner, and who had access to fewer medical and psychological services (Ullman and Filipas 2001).

Exercise: Self-Assessment—PTSD, Depression

Review the symptoms of depression and PTSD described above. On a new page in your journal entitled "Self-Assessment: PTSD," write down the symptoms of PTSD that you are experiencing. On another page, entitled "Self-Assessment: Depression," write down the symptoms of depression that you are experiencing.

If you have some of the symptoms of either of these disorders, you need professional help to determine whether you actually suffer from one of them and, if you do, to explore options to help you with the problem. Because these disorders have a biological component, few people are successful at dealing with them on their own. Medication or other forms of treatment, such as acupuncture, improved diet, and an exercise program might be needed. However, medication rarely removes all symptoms. Healing the pain behind the symptoms and learning how to empower yourself is also necessary.

Remember, aside from any hereditary or other biological factors, basically symptoms are ways of coping with the anger, loss, and sense of powerlessness that were caused by the assault. Until you deal with these feelings, even with the best of medications, symptoms can persist. It is essential, however, that the therapist you choose to help you meets the minimum criteria for effective sexual assault counseling. These criteria are listed in appendix A.

Stage III: The Reconstitution Stage

The first two stages are followed by stage III, the reconstitution stage, and then by stage IV, the resolution stage. The length of these stages varies from one woman to the next. Some women never reach stage IV. During stage III, the reconstitution stage, women try to resume their former lives. They return to work and family duties and to other pre-assault activities. Some change locks, buy a security system, get a dog, alter some of their routines, or take self-defense classes. Some change jobs, move in with relatives or friends, or relocate to another part of town, another state, or even to another country. Safety becomes a top priority for everyone.

If you had emotional reactions to the assault, you can expect those reactions to persist. If you had a controlled reaction, you may continue to be calm, or at least appear so. Perhaps you valiantly try to reclaim your life or "stay strong" for the sake of others. Perhaps you are so busy comforting and helping others with their reactions to your assault, or taking care of family emergencies, financial problems, or other stressors, that you don't have the time or emotional energy to focus on your own distress.

Outwardly it seems as if you have fully adjusted. Perhaps you have. Another possibility, however, is that underneath your surface appearance the turmoil caused by the assault is festering. Do not be surprised if, at some indefinite point in time, the confusion, pain, and any repressed self-blame and shame emerge. For some women, this will be a few weeks or months later; for others, thirty years later; for still others, never.

Alcohol and Drug Addiction and Eating Disorders

By this third stage, some survivors have developed an addiction, such as an eating disorder, drug or alcohol abuse problem, or compulsive gambling, spending, or sexual activity. If the survivor had one of these addictions before the assault, the assault may have made it much worse.

Assault survivors have been shown to be five times more likely to use prescription drugs, three times more likely to use marijuana, six times more likely to use cocaine, and ten times more likely to use other hard drugs than women who have never been assaulted. Survivors are also are twenty-six times more likely to have serious problems with drug abuse and thirteen times more likely to have serious problems with alcohol. The more vicious the rape, the more severe the alcohol problem (Department of Veterans Affairs 1993).

Addictions, whether substance abuse or compulsive spending, are deliberate ways to make yourself numb. They can consume so many of a survivor's waking hours that she doesn't have to think about the assault or any other problems in her life. Addictions also can be a form of self-medication for PTSD and depression. Alcohol, certain drugs, and excess food, for example, have been found to help regulate sleep, suppress nightmares, reduce anxiety attacks, and alleviate despair, but only for a while.

If you are using drugs or alcohol to medicate symptoms of depression or PTSD, you may find in the future that they can have a rebound effect, and your symptoms will worsen. Almost inevitably your addiction will lead to medical and financial problems that will only aggravate any problems you are already having. Ironically, addictions can create the very problems they were intended to solve. Rarely do they help a survivor cope with the assault or improve her self-esteem.

If you suspect that your spending habits, sexual activity, or alcohol, drug, and food consumption are interfering with your self-esteem, relationships, or financial and physical security, you need to consult with a trained mental health professional and follow through on her or his recommendations.

Stage IV: The Resolution Stage

During the resolution stage, some or all of the emotional, sexual, and somatic reactions may persist, but, over time, they become less intense, frequent, or disturbing. Some women reach a point where they feel as if their life is "back to normal." Yet years later, many women report feeling only partially recovered.

Some survivors never reach the fourth stage, resolution, or, if they do, they do not complete it. Once you are in this stage, you will become increasingly aware of your anger, a deep abiding rage at the assailant and any family members, friends, or medical, court, police, and mental health workers whom you feel failed to help you.

It is far healthier for you to listen to and respect your anger than to bury it or pretend it isn't there. In the long run, your mental health depends on directing your anger outward to those who deserve it rather than inward onto yourself in the form of depression, addiction, and self-destructive behaviors, such as not taking care of your health or allowing yourself to be economically or sexually exploited. Ideally, you can eventually channel your anger energy toward achieving your goals and dreams. Although using your anger energy productively does not necessarily mean that the pain of the assault will totally disappear, its claim on your energy and self-esteem will begin to subside.

Yet anger can create its own set of problems. Are you are angry about being angry? Are you confused because although one part of you is enraged, another part feels that if you contributed to the assault, even a slight bit, that you are not entitled to be so angry? Were you taught that anger is a sin or moral defect? Do you believe that "nice" girls don't get angry, or if they do, they are not supposed to show it? If so, your anger can result in guilt. If you and others around you, especially people who matter to you, do not approve of being angry, you may not feel free to express the anger you experience. As a result, when it begins to surface, you may redirect it back onto yourself.

Even if you accept your anger and have been comfortable with feeling and expressing anger in the past, you may have problems dealing with the kind of anger generated by the assault. Unless you were traumatized previously, this anger is not like the kinds of anger you have experienced before. As an anger born from trauma, it is more intense, more vicious, more enduring. Once ignited, it feels all-consuming and it doesn't go away easily.

During the assault, the threat was external, in the form of the offender. Now the threat is within, in the form of the full extent of your rage. Just as you feared being overpowered by your assailant, you may now fear being overpowered by your anger. Hence, on some level, experiencing the anger can feel like a replay of the assault, when you were not in control.

The depth of your anger is a reflection of the depth of your pain and humiliation at being powerless to protect yourself. The anger can be so great that sometimes it becomes irrational and spills over onto people who are not your real enemies. For example, Lisa became enraged at her parents, partner, teachers, and others who had a protective role in her life. Intellectually, she knew that these people had nothing to do with the assault and had been powerless to protect her, but emotionally she felt that they had failed to live up to their commitment to keep her from harm.

"It's crazy to be mad at my mom because some judge didn't believe I was really raped," said Lisa. "But the monster in me keeps telling me that she's a fake, because all her promises of love and protection were nothing but lies. I end up yelling at her over little things.

"I get paranoid sometimes, too. When I see my friends talking to each other and I can't hear what they are saying, I immediately assume they are talking against me. Even if I know it's not true, I get suspicious and so mad I want to punch them. What's happening to me? Am I losing my mind? If this goes on, I'll lose all my friends."

Sexual Effects

Sexual assault can profoundly affect a woman's sexuality and her relationship to her body. This takes on enormous importance, given that, in our culture, a woman's body and her sexuality are central to her identity. No matter what a woman has achieved at home, at work, or in the community, in our society, she still will be evaluated frequently on the basis of her appearance. Even if you completely reject the idea of women being rated according to their looks, you do live in this society. This makes it hard for you to not be affected by these cultural standards.

Has the assault made you feel dirty, ugly, or contaminated? Do you now view your sexuality as defective, bad, or evil? Do you despise and reject your body, your attractiveness, or anything to do with sex? Do you think you no longer have the "right" to be a woman? Even if the assault did not change your appearance, do you now feel less attractive and therefore devalued? Has the assault heightened any sexual issues you had prior to the assault?

You may be especially confused about your sexuality if you became sexually aroused during the assault or if afterward, you found yourself becoming excited by violent images and fantasies, by thinking or talking about the assault, or even by reading self-help and other books about sexual assault. If you blame the assault for your interest in sex, your shame and guilt might be enormous.

On the other hand, if you find yourself disinterested in sex, this does not mean you are frigid or that you have deep personality problems. Such a reaction is very common. Studies show that roughly one-third of women are estimated to stop sexual activity entirely for three months after sexual assault; another third reduce the frequency of their sexual activity. Research has also shown that up to two-thirds of women who have problems becoming aroused or having orgasm trace the beginnings of their sexual problems to a sexual assault (Becker et al. 1982). Women with histories of multiple rapes or sexual abuse as children report the most difficulties with sexual relations (van Berlo and Ensink 2000).

Some women start enjoying sex within a year after sexual assault but, for others, it takes five or six years for their sexual interest and functioning to return to what they were before the assault. Some women, however, report that even decades later, their sex lives have yet to fully recover (Koss and Harvey 1991).

In contrast, after an assault, some women begin having more sex, masturbate more frequently, watch pornography more often, or in other ways become sex-obsessed. For some of these women, this increased sexual interest might be a symbolic way of taking control of their sexuality, thus undoing the powerlessness they experienced during the assault. Sexual activity also can be a way to express anger, or to reduce it; to reduce anxiety and stress; to affirm one's sexual desirability; or to defy unsympathetic family members. It can also be a way to give yourself pleasure.

For some of these women, however, having more frequent sexual encounters is not an act of self-love, but a source of additional distress. They may think, "Why am I acting this way? Am I becoming promiscuous?" It is more likely, however, that increased sexual activity is the result of the disempowering effects of the assault. For example, sexual assault makes some women less able to refuse sexual advances or more likely to have sex just to please the other person to keep that person's affection and attention. For other women, more frequent sexual activity after the assault is an act of self-punishment or a reflection of their low self-esteem. In the words of one survivor, "Everybody thinks I'm a slut anyway, so I might as well act like one."

Common Sexual Side Effects of Sexual Assault

The sexual side effects listed here include a wide range of reactions. You may have experienced some but, probably not all, of them. Do not be surprised if your reactions are inconsistent, for example, if you avoid sexual contact for a while, become sexually active again, and then return to celibacy.

The following rather lengthy list includes the most common sexual side effects of sexual assault: feeling that one is no longer a woman or doesn't have the "right" to be a woman; fear of sexual contact, but not necessarily of hugging or holding hands; total or partial avoidance of sexual activity—or the opposite—increased sexual activity; sexual indifference or the opposite, increased sexual appetite or greater preoccupation with sex; lack of pleasure during sexual activity; difficulties becoming aroused or achieving orgasm; avoidance of sexual positions and behavior associated with the assault; fears that becoming aroused proves that "you really wanted it" or "you secretly enjoyed it"; feeling confused or inhibited, or dissociating ("tuning out" or "spacing out"); having flashbacks, fear, or anxiety during sex; fear of penetration; vaginismus (involuntary vaginal muscle spasms) in anticipation of penetration (by a man, tampon, gynecological instrument, or medication); pain (i.e., genital burning) during intercourse; increased or decreased masturbating; sudden unexplained and unwanted surges of sexual arousal; fear of losing control, or of not being able to set limits on your sexual behavior or on the sexual behavior of a partner; violent fantasies about sex during sexual activities or at other times; sexual arousal in response to violent images or images of sexual assault, or to masochistic and sadistic thoughts, images, or fantasies; indiscriminate sexual activity; if heterosexual, lesbian or bisexual desires and fantasies; if lesbian, heterosexual or bisexual desires and fantasies; sexually transmitted diseases; fear of future evidence of sexually transmitted disease even if initial test results are negative; mixed or negative feelings about any resulting pregnancy; and mixed or negative feelings about having an abortion (or not having one). Any of these sexual effects can be worsened by shame, guilt, or relationship problems stemming from the assault.

Do not conclude that having any of the reactions described here means you will never again enjoy physical intimacy. The sheer passage of time can alleviate some sexual problems. Other problems will start to lift as you begin dealing constructively with the assault through counseling or other self-help efforts, such as reading and working with this book. If your sexual problems continue to concern you, you can seek out the help of a specially trained sex therapist.

However, the process of learning to feel comfortable with your sexuality again may be stalled if you are involved in assault-related court activities; if the sexual assault resulted in the rupture of an important relationship in your life or in an interruption of your personal life goals; if you have been forced to relocate for safety reasons; if you have assault-related physical problems, such as a sexually transmitted disease, pelvic pain, or visible scars; or if you became pregnant or had an abortion.

Reclaiming your sexuality also will be difficult if you are focused almost entirely on your sexual problems. If you believe that, except for your sex life, the sexual assault did not really harm you, you are probably not yet aware of full impact of the assault. Therefore, no matter how much sex therapy you receive, if you have yet to discover the emotional impact of the assault, your sexual problems are likely to remain.

If you experience any sexual arousal or fantasies at any point while reading this book, do not be concerned. This doesn't mean you are oversexed, perverted, or permanently damaged by the assault. It simply means that an association was formed between your sexual self and an aspect of or reminder of the assault (such as reading this book, especially this particular section). This association can diminish over time.

Exercise: Sexual Effects

On a new page in your journal entitled "Impact on My Sexuality," discuss the effects of the assault on your sexual interests and activities and on your attitudes toward your sexuality. How do these effects compare with the ones discussed in this chapter?

When Circumstances Make Recovery Difficult

Unfortunately, some women live under such harsh conditions that their physical and economic survival, not their recovery from sexual assault, is their major priority. For such women, being sexually assaulted once as a adult seems inconsequential compared to other events in their lives. Laura asked, "What's a rape compared to seeing your brother murdered and losing your parents in a fire all in the same year?"

Yet, there is no doubt that for Laura, as for other women who have borne many injustices and losses, below the surface the assault eroded her sense of personal power even further. The high rates of PTSD, depression, addiction, and physical problems among survivors indicate that negative reactions are no respecter of age, class, race, or religion. Even women whose lives were not significantly disrupted by the assault can be crippled by the resulting self-doubts.

The aftereffects of sexual assault can be so severe that they can cause withdrawal from important relationships and pleasurable activities, or result in the sabotage of one's health, education, or job. For some women, life becomes focused on, if not restricted to, coping with their symptoms and little else, except what is necessary for survival.

Checking in: Return to the "Directions for Checking In" at the end of chapter 1 and answer all the questions to the best of your ability.

CHAPTER 7

Your Story and the Stages of Recovery

Recovery doesn't mean that you will never again think about the assault or have strong feelings about it. Recovery does mean that the assault will no longer direct and govern your life. It also means that despite any intrusions of your past horror into your present life, in general, you will be able to love, work, and play in a self-respecting and meaningful way. If your thoughts and feelings about the assault are grounded in realistic, as opposed to unrealistic, views of your role in what happened, you will be able to embrace the life you desire more freely and more quickly.

Recovery has two parts, the emotional, or the feelings resulting from the assault, and the mental, your view of what happened and why. Certain feelings about the assault can last a lifetime; for example, your grief for the losses you suffered. No amount of logical analysis can change that. However, the mental or cognitive part of recovery is amenable to change. A realistic appraisal of your options during the assault can help you to understand the difference between the following:

- What you legitimately can feel guilty and ashamed about (rational guilt and shame) and what you unrealistically blame yourself for or feel ashamed about (irrational guilt and shame).

- The irrevocable ways the assault has affected your life, and the ways in which this terrible experience has assumed more power over your life than is necessary.

The Stages of Recovery

Recovering from sexual assault can be divided into several stages, but it is important to remember that it is not a neat, linear process in which you complete one stage and move on to the next. Recovery from assault is more fluid than that. You may find yourself skipping a stage and coming back to it later. You also might find yourself engaged in the work of two or three stages simultaneously.

Nevertheless, the following is a simple outline of the stages involved in recovering from sexual assault.

1. Remembering what happened: You will put together the story of the assault in as much detail as you can remember, including any significant events before or after the assault took place.

2. Identifying the thoughts and feelings you had at various points during the assault.

3. Reevaluating your role in the assault in light of the total context of what was occurring before, during, and after, and in light of the common thinking errors that are discussed in detail in chapter 9. This process will help you begin separating your rational from your irrational thoughts.

4. Countering irrational negative beliefs about yourself: This involves challenging your irrational beliefs by developing positive but realistic ways of viewing the assault.

5. Seeking additional emotional healing: No matter how logically you examine your assault, some self-critical feelings may remain. Part of recovery involves working with these self-critical feelings on an emotional rather than an intellectual level. Recovery also involves accepting whatever emotional scars remain, and then finding ways to

transform their negative energy into sources for a more vital and meaningful life.

6. Seeking expert help for other concerns: If you have spiritual, medical, sexual, or other concerns, you can consult with a specialist to discuss your options.

7. Formulating realistic goals for yourself and following through on plans to change those aspects of your life over which you do have some control.

As stated above, these healing stages do not necessarily flow in a neat progression. You may find some resolution, for instance, without remembering much of what happened. Similarly, you may feel as if you have "graduated" from the recovery process, when suddenly you will arrive at a new awareness that may change almost everything you previously thought about it. Furthermore, to your surprise, the new revelation may put you back into a state of emotional pain and negativity.

Coping with Your Anger

As the result of having a more logical view of your assault, your anger at yourself will undoubtedly diminish, but your anger toward your attacker and others who have caused you emotional or physical harm will increase. Part of recovery is finding constructive uses for your anger rather than directing it outward toward people who don't deserve it or inward onto yourself.

Healing Takes Time

Healing from sexual assault can be a lifelong process. It may take months or even years to fully remember all the details, to gain perspective on it, or for the negative feelings to diminish. Your healing process will take its own course and unfold in its own time, not according to a "cookbook" recipe.

Be patient with yourself and with the process. Do not judge your efforts; just continue making them. Just as you get more out of a meal if you eat slowly and chew each bite thoroughly, it is more important to take your healing one step at a time. Do it slowly. You don't want to arrive at a superficial understanding of what happened and how it changed you.

Exercise: Attitude and Feelings toward Healing

As much as you desire recovery, a part of you may be apprehensive. All life changes, even positives ones, can be stressful. Remember, not only you, but others in your life will be adjusting to the changes in your attitude and your behavior.

In your journal on a new page entitled "My Feelings and Attitudes toward Healing," write about how recovery might affect important areas of your life, for example, your relationships, priorities, lifestyle, and spiritual beliefs. What problems do you expect? For example, are you afraid you might find out something you don't want to know? Or are you afraid that you will become too angry or too depressed, or that others might be threatened by your growth?

What joys do you anticipate? For example, do you foresee yourself becoming more assertive, successful, or creative? Do you still want to proceed? If so, why? If not, why not?

Your Story

Putting together the story of your assault is essential to your recovery. Every time you take a memory out and look at it, you change it. You may think you already remember more than you want to about the assault, or you may remember very little of it. In either case, one of the principal tools of this book (indeed as in many therapies) is to reconstruct what happened. The way to do that is to write about it.

As you write, keep in mind these three facts: (1) you will not die, explode, disintegrate, or cease to function if you dare to remember; (2) remembering will not result in the memories reoccurring as real-life events; and (3) most times the memories will eventually diminish in intensity.

If writing your entire story seems like an overwhelming task to you, then write only about two or three of the most traumatic moments. What you write at first, however, is only a beginning. As you progress doing the exercises and reading this book, you will become increasingly aware of aspects of the assault you have forgotten, and of the ways it has altered your life. Since we will return to your story several times in the remainder of this book, you will have many opportunities to add to your account. The following sections offer some suggestions to help you remember.

Remembering the Assault: Memory Aids

Talking to others, reading your story aloud, returning to the scene of the assault, reviewing police and medical reports or photos, using prompts, or reviewing any personal writing or artwork you did immediately after the assault can help to stimulate your memory.

Caution: Under no circumstance should you use any of the suggestions given here without adequate preparation or support. You must talk with your therapist or support group about your expectations and how you might feel before, during, or after using one of the memory aids described here.

For example, if you hope to find the "missing link" or the "magic answer" in your search, you may be disappointed. Even if you do discover valuable information, you may find that it doesn't take away the pain. In fact, new insights may intensify pain. In some cases, survivors have suffered long-term impairment as the result of learning more about their assault or exposing themselves to reminders of the assault, especially to the scene of the crime.

On the other hand, many survivors find that uncovering some missing pieces of their story helps to free them. Their sentiment is, "It was worth the pain to find out the truth." And if they don't find out all they hope to discover, they still feel pride in having the courage to take the risks involved in returning to the people and places of the assault.

The cautions described here are not meant to discourage you from taking an active part in your healing, but to warn you of possible negative effects. Before using any of the memory aids listed below, ask yourself if you are willing to live with the possibility of additional grief, anger, or disappointment at this point in time. If you are currently feeling vulnerable or very stressed, regardless of the reason, you may decide to use a memory aid at a later time.

Talking to Other People

If you decide to contact people who may have knowledge of you or of what happened, do not automatically assume that these people will be emotionally supportive. Even if they care about you, this doesn't mean they will be able give you the empathic listening you would expect from a trained therapist or knowledgeable survivor. When you meet with them, try to focus on your goal: gathering information. Ask neutral questions, such as, "I've been thinking lately about the assault. I've forgotten so much I'd like to remember. I wonder if you can help me recall what I was like before it happened?"

Bear in mind that seeking information from others is not the same as confronting the assailant or the officials, professionals, or others who harmed you or were not supportive. Such confrontations are complex matters well beyond the scope of this book.

Talking to other survivors, reading your story out loud to yourself, and reading about sexual assault can also stimulate your memory. Today, the topic of sexual assault is central to much of modern fiction, drama, and poetry. It is also the theme of many myths from a variety of cultures. Ask your librarian to help you find books and articles on sexual assault. (See also appendix B.)

Revisiting the Scene

Returning to the site of the assault or to the locations of any medical or judicial facilities involved is a powerful memory aid. However, it cannot be overemphasized that if you decide to do so, you must first discuss your plans with a qualified helping professional. Then you can decide together whether it is in your best interest to proceed and, if you do, how to prepare for the full range of your possible reactions to such a visit.

Using Prompts

Find photographs of yourself or significant others before or after the assault. As you look at pictures of yourself, ask yourself, "What was I like then? What did I feel like? What was I interested in?" If you are looking at pictures of others, ask yourself, "How did my relationship with this person change after the assault?"

You may wonder if it is advisable to examine pictures of your attacker or those who harmed you emotionally after the assault, for example, certain police officers, judges, medical workers, relatives, or friends. There are no hard-and-fast rules—you need to trust your gut reaction. If you don't want to look at those pictures, *don't*.

Never push yourself, and never allow others to push you, into "facing the facts" when you aren't ready or when you feel such exposure would be not only pointless but destructive to you. Sometimes it just isn't necessary to look at pictures of people or places involved in your losses, especially if the emotional price is too high to pay. You can recover without ever looking at pictures of people who have hurt you.

If you do want to look, go ahead. But it is highly recommended that you view these pictures in a supportive context, for example, with a friend or in an individual or group counseling session. Start with one picture and see how you react. If it results in too much pain or in any of the symptoms listed in the "Cautions" section of the introduction, stop immediately. You may also want to look at movies, newspapers, magazines, and objects of clothing or other artifacts, or listen to music from the year in which you were assaulted.

Writing about the Assault

The following directions will help you to write about the assault as safely as possible. The very act of taking control over the way you write about the assault can be a way to reclaim the personal power stolen from you during the assault. Respecting your feelings and your needs as you write can be healing in itself.

Directions: The following directions apply to all the exercises in this and the remaining chapters of this book where you are asked to write about your assault experience.

1. Review the "Cautions" and "How to Use This Book" sections in the introduction, and the contracts you made with yourself in chapters 1, 2, 3, and 4. Keep your phone list from chapter 3 and your safety plans from chapters 2 and 4 handy. If you haven't created a safety plan and committed to the safety precautions outlined in the first four chapters of this book, is absolutely essential that you do so now before you continue working with this chapter.

2. If you have been assaulted more than once, start with one assault only. Later on, if you choose to, you can return to these exercises and complete them for another assault.

3. Take as much time as you need for these exercises. Don't try to do them all at once. If you start feeling

overwhelmed, stop. You can always resume writing later. You may want to write for ten minutes, then take a break. It is not recommended that you not write for more than half an hour at a time. You can take several days or weeks, if necessary.

4. After you have completed a particular exercise, put your journal away for a day or two. Then reread what you have written, adding to your entries any additional memories or thoughts. Over time, your memories of the assault and your awareness of its impact will continue to sharpen and unfold. As new memories emerge, keep writing them down. If you can, keep talking about them, too.

5. Write as much or as little as you want. If you do not want to write about all that you can remember, limit your writing to the two or three most significant moments.

6. Don't be self-conscious about what you write. Your goal is to remember and record events, thoughts, and feelings—for yourself, not for others, or an English class. Let the words flow in any order or way they come to you: in phrases or single words as well as in sentences; use as many languages as you want. If you were abused as a child, parts or all of your story may come back as baby talk or as a young child might speak. If you need to draw or paint, sculpt, sing, or play music, do so, making a written notation about what you did.

7. *Memory blocks*: At various stages, you may reach memory blocks or points where you get stuck. You can't remember or think anymore, or it is simply to painful to go on. When this happens, stop. Draw a line underneath what you've written and return to it later.

8. When you've written down as much as you can, congratulate yourself for being willing to look at and deal with the assault. It takes a lot of courage.

Exercise 1: Your Story, Part One—The Assault

On a new page in your journal entitled "My Story, Part One—The Assault," describe what happened during your sexual assault;

focus on the most troublesome aspects. Include events that preceded and immediately followed the assault, especially if they are relevant to the assault or your feelings about the attack. You may want to review chapters 5 and 6 and your journal entries for those chapters, as well.

As you write, include as much sensory detail as possible, including the following:

What did the attacker(s) look like and smell like? (If there was more than one, describe each one separately, as best you can.) What did he/they say? What did he/they do? What did you say? What happened first? What did you think then? What did you feel then? What happened next? What did you think and feel then, and so forth? Were any animals, plants, or weapons involved? Were other people involved as victims, observers, or photographers? What was the season? What was the temperature? Where the did assault occur? What were the colors, textures, and smells of your clothing, the clothing of the attacker(s), and other physical objects present?

These details are important not because they are or were life-threatening in themselves but because similar details in your present life may be triggers that produce intense emotional, even physical, reactions. You may be organizing your life to avoid confronting similar details in the present. For example, Annette was assaulted after eating Chinese food. Afterward, she found herself avoiding anyone who "looked Chinese" and driving out of her way to avoid seeing and smelling Chinese restaurants.

Be as specific as possible, not only about the sensory details, but about your feelings, especially your fears. For example, if you were sexually aroused by the attack or fantasized about torturing the attacker, at least note these reactions mentally. You don't have to write them down if you don't want to. And you don't ever have to tell anybody. You only need to acknowledge them to yourself. Hopefully, someday you will not feel guilty about any of your reactions.

Exercise 2: Your Story, Part Two— How the Assault Affected Your Life

On a new page in your journal entitled "My Story, Part Two— How the Assault Affected My Life," describe how the assault affected various parts of your life. Consider the impact of the assault on the following: your faith in the world and yourself, your relationships, your vocation, and your ability to calm yourself without a mood-altering substance such as food, drugs, or alcohol.

You may want to itemize your financial, emotional, medical, or physical losses and, if applicable, your philosophical, spiritual, or moral losses. Take some time to complete this exercise: It's far more important than it may appear at first.

Financial costs. Make a list of the financial losses you sustained as a result of the assault. Consider both direct and indirect costs. Direct costs include money or property that were stolen, medical and mental health bills, relocation expenses, legal fees, babysitting and transportation costs (to go to court, doctor's appointments, and so on), and days lost from work. Also include any financial costs borne by relatives, friends, religious or charitable institutions, or anonymous donors.

Indirect costs include the cost of lost opportunities, for example, loss of career opportunities you were unable to pursue due to psychological or other conditions stemming from the assault. Perhaps you had to go to court several times, and while you were busy with the court system, you missed out on applying for a new job or a promotion. That's an indirect cost.

Emotional costs. From what assault-related emotional symptoms have you suffered and for how long? How have you had to limit social, vocational, and other aspects of your life because of these symptoms or because of negative responses from people who matter to you or those who have power over your life? These are all losses. What emotional costs did your family members and friends have to bear? Were they also stigmatized or rejected?

About how many hours have you and your loved ones suffered because of the assault? If you were paid minimum wage for all those hours, how much money would you have for all those hours of suffering?

Medical and physical costs. Did the assault harm any of your physical or mental abilities? If so, list which ones and how they were damaged. Have these physical and mental limitations negatively affected other aspects of your life: your job, relationships, sex life, creative pursuits, and so on? If so, explain how.

Philosophical, spiritual, and moral costs. What cherished beliefs about yourself, specific people, specific groups, organizations, or institutions, and people in general, were negatively affected by the assault? Be as specific as possible in your listing.

You can also ask yourself, "How would my life be different if I had never been assaulted? What would I be doing, feeling, and thinking differently?" If there were any positive effects of the assault, include those as well.

As you write, you may become more keenly aware of your losses, anger, and fear. Remember to stop as needed and use your phone list and safety plans as often as necessary.

Exercise 3: Your Life— Before and after the Assault

You can get a clearer look at the impact the assault had by making a before and after chart for various aspects of your life. On a new page in your journal entitled "My Life—Before and after the Assault," draw three columns. Label the first column "Aspect of Life," the second "Before the Assault," and the third "After the Assault."

Under the "Aspect of Life "column, make a vertical list of the different areas of life listed below. Note that this exercise will require several pages. Leave plenty of room so you can add information later. Feel free to leave out those categories that do not apply to you and add other categories if you wish. Review and use your journal entry for the previous exercise as you complete this exercise.

Aspect of Life	Before the Assault	After the Assault
1. Finances		
2. Health and health habits		
3. Fears		
4. Sexuality		
5. Intimate relationships		
6. Relationships with children		
7. Relationships with family of origin		

8. Relationships with neighbors or community

9. Participation in church or other organizations

10. Psychological symptoms

11. Sleeping patterns

12. Eating patterns

13. Alcohol and drug use

14. Gambling, spending

15. Recreation

16. Mental abilities: memory, concentration, analysis

17. Trust in the world

18. Trust in self and sense of personal power

19. Work performance and career goals (includes homemakers)

20. Relationships with coworkers, supervisors, and so forth

21. Other _____ (add as many categories as you wish)

In the Before and After columns, write short descriptions of how you were before and after the assault for each category.

Checking in: Return to the "Directions for Checking In" at the end of chapter 1 and answer all the questions to the best of your ability.

CHAPTER 8

Reconstructing the Assault—Part One: Thoughts and Feelings

Your thoughts and feelings are intimately related. The way you think about a situation affects your emotional response to it and vice versa. For example, if your doctor refers you to a specialist and you view the referral as a personal rejection, you may feel humiliated or angry. However, if you view it as the doctor's effort to take better care of you, you will feel pleased.

Similarly, the way you think about your sexual assault can profoundly affect its emotional impact on your life. The more rationally you are able to view the assault, by taking into account the numerous factors that were involved, the more your self-blame and other negative feelings will begin to diminish.

Of course, a more rational view does not mean you will (or "should") be able to "think away" all of your strong feelings about the assault. In this chapter and chapter 9, you will be asked to mentally reconstruct the assault so that you can come to view it more rationally. This will involve a series of steps that build on each other. Therefore, *it is important to complete the exercises for each of these steps in the order in which they appear. These exercises are crucial to your recovery.* However, they are difficult because they require you to think hard about your assault. For that reason, you may need to take more breaks and that is also the reason these exercises are spread over two chapters.

Prepare for Possible Anger and Grief

No amount of logical analysis can erase your painful memories. However, the more realistically you can come to view the assault, the more you may come to appreciate that you were not *as responsible* for what happened as you may have thought previously. You may also see more clearly how certain other people or organizations played a larger role than you had thought. These insights could decrease your anger toward yourself and create or increase your fury at others. *The intensity of your anger may surprise you.* If you need help managing your anger, use the safety plans you created in chapters 3 and 4 or consult appendix B. Additional exercises for anger are provided in chapter 10.

As you become increasingly able to view your assault more rationally, your feelings of helplessness and grief may also grow stronger. Feeling guilty feels awful, but grieving or feeling helpless can feel worse. At least feeling guilty allows you to believe that you have some control over your life. But during the assault you had little control, if any. Therefore, as your guilt and shame lessen, your awareness of your vulnerability and your losses may increase. The resulting pain can be excruciating. Consult appendix B for help in dealing with feelings of helplessness and grief, or contact the medical and mental health professionals and organizations you identified in the safety contract you created in chapter 3.

Writing Your Story (One More Time)

In this chapter you will be asked to write your story once again. You may wonder (justifiably) "Why do I have to write about those horrible moments over and over again?" There are three reasons for this:

1. The more times you write or think about the assault, the more aspects of it you may remember. Uncovering certain details has spared many a survivor decades of misery. For example, some women suppress the attacker's threats to harm them if they fought back. By reworking their story several times, however, these women may recall those threats. This new information helps them to forgive themselves for not having resisted more forcefully.

2. Reviewing the assault repeatedly can lessen its power. When working with survivors, Resick (1994) asks them to read their story *out loud for two weeks*. Usually the more the assault is talked about openly, the less frightening it becomes. There are some exceptions, however. *If revisiting the assault leads to any of the symptoms listed in the "Cautions" section of the introduction to this book, you need to stop immediately and seek help.*

3. Although you will be writing your story again, you will not do so as you did before, or for the same purpose. This time you will be scrutinizing what happened from the point of view of an objective observer. Also, you will be looking not only at your physically observable actions, but the actions of your heart and mind—your thoughts and feelings. Your thoughts and feelings are just as real and important as behaviors that others can see or hear.

Although you may think of the assault as a single event, there were multiple events within that event and, therefore, many possibilities for generating or confirming irrational beliefs and negative feelings. You may have had *one* thought prior to a particular act, *another* thought (or more) during it, and a *different* thought afterward. The same holds true for feelings: You might have had several feelings before, during, and after particular acts. Furthermore, it may be what you *didn't* do, think, or feel that is contributing to your agony. So you need to look at what you actually did, thought, or felt, and what you didn't do, think, or feel.

It is important to become aware of as many of your reactions as possible. All too often, survivors focus only on those few reactions that cause them shame and guilt and they give little weight to those reactions they find acceptable. For example, one woman was fixated on the memory of how elated she felt when her attacker kissed her. To her, and to some others, this meant she had provoked the assault. However, she had forgotten the other feelings she had felt for him: her disgust at his lewd remarks and her fear of his aggression. Furthermore, her loathing and terror were every bit as strong, if not stronger than her few moments of sexual excitement.

Reconstructing the Assault

Open your journal to five new pages. Across the top of each new page write a title. The first page should be entitled "What Happened"; the second, "Reactions—Thoughts, Feelings, and Beliefs"; the third, "Separating Assault-Related Feelings from Other Emotional Issues"; the fourth, "Identifying Sources of Assault-Related Negative Feelings"; and the fifth page, "Thinking Errors."

Be sure to leave sufficient space before and after each entry so that you can insert any new thoughts, feelings, or actions that you recall while you work on these exercises. When you finish this chapter and have taken a break, you will complete this set of exercises in chapter 9 with two more exercises called "Looking at the Big Picture—A More Rational View," and "Know Your Strengths."

Exercise 1: What Happened

In this exercise you will record the assault by breaking it down into a detailed chronological account. On page 1, describe what happened first, then what happened next, what happened after that, and so on. Be sure to include your thoughts and feelings at the time, as well as your behaviors. Also, record what you did *not* do, think, or feel, the memory of which may have harmed your self-esteem. Then write a number beside each entry so you can refer to it easily in the four exercises in this chapter and the two exercises in chapter 9.

Reminder: Before you begin this exercise, review "Writing about the Assault" in chapter 7, and reread your journal entries for the exercises you completed in that chapter on writing your story.

Example: Judy's Story

Judy and Peter both loved Bates Park. Even though it was located in the middle of the city, its waterfall and rocky hills made them feel as if they were in a forest. To avoid the afternoon crowds, they decided to meet there early one Sunday morning. Judy arrived promptly at 8 A.M., but Peter was not there. She phoned him repeatedly; but each time, got no reply. Around 9 A.M., he called her on her cell phone. He had overslept and would be there in an hour. "If I'm not in the car, I'll be at the waterfall," she told him. Shortly after she reached the falls, someone came up behind her and punched her in the back. She screamed. Then he gagged her mouth, pulled her into a crevice, and sexually assaulted her.

When Peter found Judy dazed and bleeding, he thought she had slipped on the rocks. "I was attacked," she whispered. Peter wanted to go to a hospital or police station immediately, but all Judy wanted was to go home. Three weeks later, she decided to report the assault.

One officer was sympathetic, but another one asked, "Why did you wait so long to report it? Lady, rapes don't usually happen on Sunday mornings, not in public places like that park. If it happened the way you say it did, near the waterfall, why didn't you shove him? Those rocks are so slippery, he would have tripped at least." Turning to Peter, he said, "Have you two been fighting lately? Is she trying to get your sympathy or to get back at you for something?"

Because it was too late for a physical inspection, and Judy could have acquired her injuries from falling on the rocks, there was no "real" evidence other than Judy's word. The officers were not even sure whether Judy's complaint could be officially recorded as a sexual assault. After the police left, Peter cursed the officer who had implied that Judy had lied. Yet the officer's accusation had planted a seed of doubt deep inside Peter's mind because a week before the assault, Peter had told Judy that he wanted to postpone their wedding because of certain issues.

Judy had burst into tears and vowed to do anything to save their relationship. They had decided to meet at the park to talk things over. Now, Judy's greatest fear was that Peter would see her as she saw herself: as "damaged goods," unsuitable to marry. In the months after the rape, her nightmares and vaginal pain brought their sex life to a halt. Judy blamed herself for not being able to "get back to normal." But she also blamed Peter. She kept thinking that if only he hadn't overslept that day, the rape would never have happened.

Peter felt guilty, too, not just for being late, but for having doubted Judy's account of what had happened. Yet he was also irritated with her. He could understand her distress immediately after the rape, but after a few months had passed, he couldn't understand why she was still so depressed and anxious. Because they both felt guilty and angry, they had many misunderstandings and conflicts, all of which only intensified Judy's despair.

Judy wrote Exercise 1: "What Happened" as follows:

1. Driving to the park, I felt anxious because Peter and I weren't getting along the way we used to.

2. I thought about being with Peter in the park and telling him how much I loved him.

3. I fantasized about having sex with Peter. This made me happy and a little excited.

4. I got to the park exactly on time and waited in the car for Peter for an hour.

5. By 9 A.M., I had called him ten times, but all I got was his answering service. I didn't know whether to be mad at him for being late or to be scared that maybe he had been hurt.

6. I thought about leaving the following message on his answering service, but I didn't: "If something happens to me while I'm waiting for you, it will all be your fault. Then you'll be sorry for postponing our wedding because of your stupid issues."

7. After Peter called, I was still upset with him, but mainly I was relieved that he was safe.

8. I was so agitated that I decided to walk to the waterfall. I thought that maybe the exercise and listening to the water would help me to calm down. I didn't want to be upset when Peter and I had our talk.

9. On the way to the waterfall, I noticed that nobody was around. I wondered if it was safe to be walking alone. But I had never heard of anyone being attacked in Bates Park.

10. At the waterfall, someone grabbed me from behind and knocked me down.

11. I thought about poking his eyes out with my fingers, but I was afraid this could make him even more brutal. I thought about shoving him, too, but all of a sudden I had no strength.

12. He pinned me down and raped me.

Memory Block

13. The next thing I remember is Peter carrying me to his car.

Memory Block

14. Peter and I argued a lot and I had a lot of awful headaches.

Judy could recall many of her thoughts, feelings, and actions prior to the assault and for several weeks afterwards. But her account of the moment-to-moment details of the most fear-provoking aspects of the assault was extremely sketchy. Whenever she tried to describe these parts, she became nauseous and dizzy. Obviously, she had reached a memory block.

Memory Blocks

Memory blocks can occur when the emotions associated with part of a woman's assault experience are so terrorizing or painful that she feels she won't be able to manage them. They also can occur when some aspect of her assault experience challenges a cherished belief or ideal. This can create a mental or moral dilemma which the woman may feel is unresolvable.

Judy, for example, could not reconcile her view of herself as a strong, responsible woman with what she now judged as her reckless behavior (walking to the waterfall alone) and her inadequate efforts at self-defense. Neither could she reconcile her view of herself as an emotionally stable person with the post-assault mood swings and other symptoms she was having. Furthermore, she had been taught to "Watch what you pray for. You might get it." Yet she had impulsively wished to be harmed so Peter would be sorry about postponing their wedding. She knew that wishing wasn't exactly like praying, but it was close enough for her to believe that she had brought the assault upon herself.

These ideas (and the feelings that accompanied them) caused Judy so much anguish that she couldn't bear to think about them, much less put them on paper. Yet with the help of a therapist, she began to make some progress in dissecting what had happened that terrible morning. For example, using her list from "Exercise 1: What Happened" she was able to record a few additional events, including the following:

Item 3. When I had sexual fantasies about Peter, I also fantasized about my ex-boyfriend. To me, that proves that, unconsciously, I'm really a slut, which is why Peter may not marry me. It also shows that the rapist could have picked up on my sexual vibes, and that's why the assault occurred.

Item 4. Before Peter called, I waited in the car for an hour, because, even though it was Sunday morning, I wondered if the park was safe. I should never have gotten out of the car.

Item 9. On the way to the waterfall, I got scared again, and I even thought about going back and locking myself in the car. But then I told myself that I had probably been watching too many movies. This was the second time I didn't pay attention to my intuition. How foolish can a woman be?

Some of these later revelations caused Judy to feel the most shame and guilt. The same may be true for you: What is hardest to think or write about may hold the clue to the sources of some of your deepest pain. It is understandable for you to want to bury your memories of certain humiliating and fearful moments. However, by doing so you may overlook facts closely associated with those moments that could provide you the relief you need. Even if such liberating information does not exist, denying your fears only enhances their power. The more you can confront them, the more you can take back the power they have exerted over your life.

It may seem like overkill to you, but it is well worth your while to go back and review what you have written once again and even read it out loud (or to a therapist). Then ask yourself if you have left out anything. Add any additional details that you remember. These details may help you heal.

For example, in having the courage to review some of the events that had caused her so much shame, Judy was able to uncover additional information that helped restore her self-esteem. For instance, when she reviewed item 3, she recalled that she had fantasized about Peter for almost ten minutes, but about her ex-boyfriend only for a few seconds. This recollection helped her to see that she was not a "slut," and that she was ready for the commitment of marriage.

By reviewing item 4, Judy suddenly remembered that while she was waiting for Peter in her car, a park ranger had come by on a horse. He had smiled and waved at her, implying that all was well. Also, en route to the waterfall she had observed and noted an emergency phone station. These additional details helped her to appreciate that she had not been as reckless or foolhardy as she had thought.

Doing the hard work of going over her story again revealed yet another detail that helped Judy to reduce and ease her sense of shame. During the assault, her attacker had said to her, "See, you're wet. I knew you were the kind who likes sex with strangers." This remark was doubly humiliating because in her past Judy had slept with a near-stranger. For a split second, she wondered if the assault was a "punishment" for that affair or even, perhaps, if her attacker was the man from her past. When she recalled what the attacker had said to her, she also recalled, with great relief, that two men looked nothing like each other.

That split-second sense of guilt was largely unconscious until Judy completed this exercise. Even though it was a relatively minor guilt feeling, it had contributed to her self-hatred. The nagging sense of "There was something else I did wrong," that had haunted her for so long now had a name: the "something else" was her past flirtation.

By identifying her guilt in the light of day (rather than burying it), Judy was able to see her past affair for what it had been—a brief safe-sex fling—with no long-term harmful consequences, instead of what she had begun to suspect it to be—proof that she was hopelessly promiscuous and, therefore, had both attracted and deserved the assault.

The more painful your feelings, the more you see your thoughts and feelings as being socially unacceptable; and the more internal and interpersonal conflicts caused by the assault, the more likely it is that you will struggle as you complete this exercise. If you are blocked in recalling your thoughts, feelings, or other details of the rape, or if you are unwilling to record them; if your account sounds more like a lab report than the drama that it was; or if you find yourself skimming over certain events or minimizing certain thoughts or feelings you experienced, like Judy, you may need professional help. The guidance and support of a qualified therapist can be very helpful in aiding you to uncover extremely stressful memories about aspects of the assault.

Exercise 2: Reactions— Thoughts, Feelings, and Beliefs

For each entry you made for Exercise 1, record the thoughts and feelings you have right now about those entries on the second page, under the title, "Reactions—Thoughts, Feelings, and Beliefs." First, consider your thoughts and beliefs. How do you view your various actions, thoughts, and feelings? Do you see them as reasonable, unreasonable, admirable, or as something else? Then consider your feelings. How do you feel about each particular action, thought, or feeling? Does it make you feel proud, sad, fearful, or ashamed, or do you have some other feeling? You may have more than one thought or feeling about each item on your list. If so, write down all of them. Even if some of them contradict each other, be sure to list them all. Notice that when Judy did Exercise 2 she was able to add more to each item on her original list of "What Happened."

1. I'm mad at myself for having been so nervous about meeting with Peter. If only I wasn't so insecure and had more self-confidence, like my sister Lisa, I would never have been in that park that day. When Peter brought up the idea of meeting at Bates Park on Sunday morning, I told him I wanted to meet another time because I was going to be helping a friend to move on Saturday, and I'd probably be too tired to get up early on Sunday to meet him. But Peter frowned and said that time was the best for him, so I dropped the matter. I guess I also wanted to prove to him that our relationship was my top priority.

   Lisa told me, "If you start giving into him now, what will it be like after you're married? Find a time that's convenient for both of you, not just him. He might not like you're standing up for yourself, but he'll respect you for it later." If I had been strong enough to follow her advice, I would have never been assaulted.

2. What if my attacker had been following me in his car? If I had been watching the road instead of thinking about Peter, I might have spotted him, and the rape would never have happened. Peter was on my mind when I left home too. That's why I forgot my hiking boots. If I had been wearing my boots when I was on those rocks, I'd have had better balance and I might have been able to shove that creep down the rocks. Lisa is right: I shouldn't let any man, not even Peter, be so important to me.

3. Thinking about having sex with Peter aroused me. Remembering my old boyfriend made me feel sexual too. I had even started to lubricate. How embarrassing. I know I spent more time daydreaming about Peter than about my ex, but how can I say I love Peter when I'm still thinking about my ex? Something must be wrong with me. I must have a wild streak. That proves that deep inside I'm not the respectable woman everyone thinks I am. I'm really a bad, too lustful, too out-of-control woman. Maybe Peter sensed this and that's why he's not sure about marrying me.

   It was probably my sexual vibes from all my fantasies that attracted the rapist. I used to feel so superior to women who brag about how many men they've been with, and who sleep with almost anybody. But now I see that I'm just like they are—a slut. I probably deserved to be raped, to teach me a lesson, to stick with one man.

4. I shouldn't have waited in that car for a whole hour. That made me too restless, and I just had to go take that damned walk. *I should have left right after the park ranger came by.* After he waved at me, he turned around and headed for the exit. At the time, I thought that meant everything was safe in the park, so he wasn't needed. But his leaving really *was* a sign that I should leave the park too. But numbskull that I am, I didn't get the message.

5. I became agitated and I started resenting the power Peter had over me.

6. I'm glad I had the self-control not to leave that message for Peter. But even thinking about leaving such a message shows me that somewhere deep inside, I wished the

assault to happen. I should know better than to make such wishes.

Once in grade school I wanted the lead part in a skit, but another girl was chosen. I was so jealous I wished something bad would happen to her. A few days later she fell off her bike and had to stay in the hospital a week. So, I know that wishing has power. Maybe I wished for the assault to make Peter realize how important I am to him or maybe I'm just a sick person. And if the opposite is true, that I didn't wish for the assault to happen, then why didn't I go home right then?

7. More proof that I'm not assertive enough: I wanted to tell Peter how angry I was at his being so late. I bet Lisa wouldn't have thought twice about telling Peter if she was mad at him. But Lisa is prettier than me. Everyone says so, even my parents. If some man doesn't like her speaking her mind, she can always find another one. Maybe if I was prettier or had a Barbie-doll figure, I'd be more assertive too. I'm so jealous of her, but it's wrong to be so jealous. She can't help it if she was born beautiful and I wasn't, and she really cares about me too.

8. If I had brought a magazine with me, I might have been content to stay in the car. If I needed to calm down, I could have called a friend or listened to music. My mom's right, I should learn to be more patient, like my sister.

9. Stupid me. I should have paid attention to my fear and turned around. Stupid me again. I was so agitated I didn't pay attention to my surroundings. I could have at least had the cell phone on me, so I could have called the police. If the rapist had seen me carrying the cell phone, maybe he would have left me alone. I could have even called a friend and asked her to stay on the line until Peter got there, just in case I needed help.

10. I hate myself for never having taken a self-defense course. I should have at least remembered those self-defense techniques I'd read about a few weeks ago. I'd even practiced them a few times. With such a bad memory, I'll never get ahead in life.

11. Failed again. The one self-defense technique I did finally manage to remember—the eye-poking one—I was too scared to try. Couldn't I have at least tried to shove him off me? He wasn't that big. I thought I was in pretty good shape, but I guess I'm a weakling.

12. I did try to get him off of me, but the rocks were cutting into my back. If I'd been braver about the pain, maybe I could've put up more of a fight. Then he might have been afraid of losing his balance and falling down on the rocks, and he might've let me go. I'm such a wimp. No wonder the kids used to laugh at me in grade school.

   I'm the only one I know who needs three shots of anesthesia to get a cavity filled. Mom says it's because I don't eat right, and my sister thinks I do it for attention. Now they say I'm having nightmares to get attention, and to make Peter feel sorry for me and stay with me.

13. This part is still a blur, but that's the part that scares me. What did I say in front of Peter? On television you see women blurting out all kinds of secrets when they're in a lot of pain. Did I do that? Did I say mean things or talk about another man? Did I confess to things I'm ashamed of? Is that why Peter and I are having so many problems now?

14. Peter has every right to still be mad at me for not going to a hospital or calling the police right after I was raped. If I had, maybe the police would've believed me when I tried to tell them later, and maybe then they would have caught the rapist. Now he's probably off attacking other women, and that's my fault. I was too much of a coward to come forward when I should have.

   I shouldn't be having all these headaches or any other symptoms either. My bruises weren't that bad. I didn't have much vaginal tearing either because, and this is the shame of shames, I was already partly lubricated when he attacked me. So why is sex so hard for me? If this keeps up I'm going to lose everything, Peter, my family, my friends, my career plans, and it's all my fault!

Exercise 3: Separating Assaulted-Related Feelings from Other Emotional Issues

Sexual assault creates its own pain. However, like any life-changing event, it can bring to the surface unresolved issues you had prior to the assault. You may, therefore, be coping with two levels of pain: pain originating from the assault and pain originating from the intensification of earlier issues in your life. In the following exercise, you will begin to separate the negative feelings and beliefs generated by the assault from those that are more directly related to your other life experiences.

For example, while driving to the park, Judy had thought about her dog's death the year before. In this instance, it is clear that that loss, although part of Judy's assault experience, was not directly related to the attack. In other instances, however, Judy's reactions were related both to the assault and to her earlier life experiences. For instance, when the police officer implied that she was lying about being raped, she felt particularly hurt and angry. His accusation was especially painful because Judy's mother had often unfairly called her a "liar" and compared her in other unfavorable ways to her sister, Lisa, who was called "the angel."

As you complete Exercise 3, you will undoubtedly discover emotional issues related both to the assault and to earlier events in your life. Do not try to assess how much of your pain is due to the assault as compared to an earlier event. All that matters is for you to recognize that a particular aspect of the assault may have affected you more deeply because it is similar to a distressing event in your past.

Begin this exercise by reviewing your journal entries on page 2 "Reactions—Thoughts, Feelings, and Beliefs." Then, go to page 3, "Separating Assaulted-Related Feelings from Other Emotional Issues." Make a list of the various types of feelings you experienced, for example, guilt, self-doubt, shame, fear, rage, numbness, or confusion. Leave plenty of space between each item that you list.

Judy's entries on this page included the following:

- **Anger at Peter:** I felt Peter was selfish in not being willing to change the time of the meeting, but then he's always been that way. He assumes that his schedule is more important than mine. I'm angry that he overslept. If I had overslept, he would have had a fit. I'm angry that he's not more understanding about how bad I feel or why it's hard for me to have sex with him.

- **Jealousy of Lisa:** I'm jealous of her self-confidence, good looks, and assertiveness.

- **Anxiety:** I doubt my ability to keep Peter and my ability to find another relationship if Peter and I break up. I doubt my ability to be responsible for myself, like not having studied self-defense. I doubt my memory and my ability to stand up for myself, to make good decisions, and to be alert to danger.

- **Self-doubt:** I doubt my inner worth and my morality. I doubt my mental and emotional stability. I had some insecurities before the assault, but now it feels as if they've multiplied a hundred times. Now I have new insecurities, like doubting my ability to make good decisions.

- **Guilt:** I feel guilty about not having been more assertive with Peter, about not paying attention to my fear, and about going limp.

- **Shame:** I felt and still feel ashamed of my sexuality, my anger, and my jealousies.

For each emotional issue you list, write a sentence or two about how that issue is related to having been sexually assaulted. If the emotional issue is not related to the assault, write a sentence or two about the origins of that issue. This is a very difficult exercise. Take some time to think before you reply and be sure to reward yourself when you are finished.

For example, under "self-doubt," Judy also wrote: "I know it doesn't make sense, but I feel that my self-doubts caused the rape. If I hadn't feel so insecure about Peter's commitment to me, I probably would have put my foot down about when to meet at the park. Because I feel guilty about not being good enough for Peter, I try to make it up to him by giving in to him when I shouldn't." Under "jealousy," she wrote: "My jealousy of Lisa goes way back, but that doesn't have anything to do with what happened. I have to keep my guilt about being jealous of her and my anger that I'm not more attractive separate from my guilt about the rape."

Exercise 4: Identifying Sources of Assault-Related Negative Feelings

You should now be able to distinguish negative feelings that were caused by the assault, either in full or in part, and those that are related to other situations and events. Return to your entries on page 2 and for every entry that involves guilt, shame, or another negative feeling related to the assault, write a statement that connects your negative feeling with that aspect of the assault. Include those instances where the negative feeling is related both to the assault and to an earlier life experience.

Here are some of Judy's entries for this exercise:

Item 4. I feel guilty about being willing to tolerate the emotional and physical stress of waiting in the car that long, because that shows I'm too dependent on Peter, and because the waiting led me to the walk that led to my rape. I also feel guilty for not having realized that when the ranger left the park, that was a sign that I should leave the park.

Item 10. I feel ashamed that I couldn't remember any of the self-defense techniques I had read about or even the few that I practiced.

Item 11. I feel guilty because I wasn't brave enough to try to poke out his eyes. I feel guilty for not having the strength to shove him off of me. I feel guilty for not taking vitamins, for not exercising more, and for not taking the self-defense class that was offered at the gym a few months ago.

Item 14. I am ashamed of being such a psychological wreck. I feel guilty because I can't make myself stop thinking or having nightmares about the rape. I can't even pretend to enjoy being intimate with Peter because I blame him for what happened, when it really wasn't his fault. I feel guilty because I'm so sensitive and overreact to everything, which causes lots of fights with Peter. I feel guilty for having headaches because headaches are caused by psychological problems, and if I could only get a grip on myself I'd be okay.

Now, take a break. Doing these four exercises can be emotionally draining and you need to stop for a while.

When you return from your break, go to chapter 9 and begin reading the descriptions and illustrations of thinking errors. This theoretical digression is necessary if you want to understand how Judy finally healed herself. Her healing had everything to do with learning how to analyze her patterns of thought. With the aid of a trusted counselor, Judy examined all her thoughts for their internal logic and relation to the world, and she found them wanting.

By using the thinking errors in chapter 9 as her guide, Judy was able to change how she thought about the experience of being raped and disbelieved. Her feelings of shame, guilt, and self-hatred lifted and were replaced with self-acceptance and a deeper love for herself than she had ever known. You can make such changes, too.

But before you can analyze your thinking properly, you need to become aware of the most common thinking errors. If you want to know how Judy worked with these thinking errors to come to her own conclusions about her sexual assault, you can skip to the section in chapter 9 entitled "How Judy Used Common Thinking Errors." You can then return to the beginning of the chapter to learn about the thinking errors and begin to apply them to your own experience.

CHAPTER 9

Reconstructing the Assault—Part Two: Common Thinking Errors

At one time or another, most people draw conclusions or make decisions without having enough information or without considering all of the relevant factors. At times their thinking may be distorted, even irrational. But this doesn't mean they lack intelligence or aren't trying hard enough to sort things out.

Often their thinking processes are influenced by certain false assumptions of which they are not aware. These hidden assumptions, or thinking errors, are so widespread and cause so much human misery that, in the past few decades, many psychologists have studied them to learn how they work and what their impact is on emotional and mental health.

The following descriptions of the common thinking errors discussed here rely heavily on the contributions of other therapists and trauma specialists who have written extensively on helping people sort out their rational thoughts and beliefs from their irrational ones. For you, as for other assault survivors, familiarity with these cognitive errors will help you to challenge the self-doubts generated by the assault.

1. Hindsight bias. When you believe that you could have known what was going to happen *before* it was possible to know it, you are indulging in hindsight bias. It also means believing that you overlooked certain "signs," such as a thought, feeling, or dream or another person's intuition, comment, or dream, that "signaled" you would soon be attacked. Yet, if you hadn't been violated, you may have never regarded those alleged "omens" as definitive information. You most likely would have forgotten them or dismissed them as superstitions (Kubany 1997).

For example, one evening Rachel had a "bad feeling" about going to class. The day before, a student had been raped in the campus parking lot. The offender had not been caught. Yet an exam review was scheduled for that evening and the university had promised to increase its security measures. Rachel reasoned that the rapist wouldn't be so foolish as to return the scene of the crime with so many security officers on duty. So she went to the classroom for the review.

While she was gone, a man broke into her car and hid on the floor of the backseat. When Rachel returned, he forced her to drive to a motel. There he raped her and deliberately broke her arm.

Today, Rachel blames herself for the assault because she believes that she should have known that the rapist would return. Yet she had no knowledge of what would happen that evening and she was confident that the university would provide adequate security. She also feels guilty she didn't pay attention to her "bad feeling" and stay at home. Yet most people base their actions on high probability outcomes, not low probability, which is the standard for hunches, intuitive feelings, or premonitions.

Sometimes people view the thoughts, dreams, or intuitions they had before a terrible event as omens because this gives them an illusion of control over events where they had little or no control (Kubany and Manke 1995). Some people even alter their memories of an event to include premonitions. It may be less painful for them to blame themselves for not paying attention to these signs than to feel powerless (Terr 1983).

2. Confusing the possibility that you could have prevented the assault with the belief that you caused it. Often hindsight bias leads to the mistaken belief that if you "could somehow have prevented" the assault, that means you "actually caused it" (Kubany 1997). For example, if Rachel had gone along with her "bad feeling" and stayed home, she would not have been attacked in the parking lot. But that does not mean she caused the assault.

3. Failing to consider or accept this truth: Certain scientifically proven, involuntary, emotional and biological reactions to trauma or extreme stress are so powerful they cannot be controlled by personal determination or willpower. Under extremely stressful conditions, such as the anticipatory and impact stages of sexual assault, time is limited and confusion reigns. After an assault, there is seldom the luxury of extended fact-gathering, consultation with experts, and careful weighing of options (Kubany 1997). In addition, extreme stress can result in biologically based reactions such as dissociation or adrenaline surges that can impair mental abilities. (See chapters 2, 4, 5, and 6.)

For example, during the assault Rachel tried desperately to think of ways to escape. Yet, her terror had triggered an adrenaline surge that interfered with her ability to concentrate. "What was wrong with me? I couldn't even think!" she lamented later. If Rachel persists in blaming herself for her body's involuntary reactions to life-threatening situations, then she is making a serious error that can interfere with her healing.

4. Evaluating what you did based on information you discovered after the assault, or based on options you thought of *after* the rape. It isn't fair to judge yourself about the decisions you made during a devastating assault by considering options that you thought of later, after you had some time to think about what you could have done differently, or after you've brainstormed with others (Kubany 1997). You can weigh the merits of what you did only against the alternatives you thought of at the time, not those that you thought of later. For example, Rachel felt guilty for not having asked campus security or a classmate to walk her to her car. If she had, perhaps the assault would not have occurred. However, she thought of those options only after the assault.

5. Judging your actions against improbable options not found in the real world. Kubany (1997) writes that it isn't fair for you to judge yourself for what you did or didn't do against idealistic impossible choices. Although we all wish for a miracle or pray for a magic rescuer to save us from a horrible situation, the unhappy reality is that there are situations when it's impossible to stop the violence. Judging your actions against what someone with super-human abilities could have done is called "superman" or "super-woman" guilt.

For instance, in the past, whenever Rachel had thought about sexual attacks, she had thought she would be able to sub-due the attacker with the self-defense techniques she had seen in adventure movies. Yet she had never practiced any of these tech-niques, many of which are beyond any person's physical abilities, regardless of their training.

6. Catch-22 guilt. Most sexual assaults are "lose-lose" situations, where all of the woman's choices are unacceptable. The option of ensuring the well-being of all concerned or of remaining true to all of her personal values does not exist. Her best choice is, alas, the one with the least negative consequences (Kubany 1997).

For example, suppose the victimized woman is a nun, and she has to choose between losing a limb or performing a sex act that she considers lewd and immoral. She must decide which option is the least horrible.

7. Judging yourself based on what happened rather than on what you intended to happen. You may feel guilty about some-thing you did, thought, or felt because the outcome was unexpectedly disastrous (Kubany 1997). But you need to judge yourself on the basis of what you *intended* to happen, not what *actually* happened. For example, it would be irrational for Rachel to feel guilty about having gone to school the night she was assaulted because her goal was to go to class, not to be victimized.

Another example is that of a woman who agrees to have oral sex with a man she has dated several times, but who wants to post-pone having sexual intercourse with him until they decide to be sexually monogamous. Her date may respect her wishes initially, but later he may force himself on her. Afterward she may feel she caused the assault because she agreed to have oral sex with him.

But her intention was to have sexual contact within certain limits, not to abandon her limits, nor to have them violated. She is not responsible for the fact that her date may act out of commonly held sexist beliefs: such as, that a woman's "no" means "yes"; that if a woman engages in some form of sexual activity that means she is also willing to engage in other forms of sexual activity; or that a woman who is a "tease" deserves to be sexually overpowered.

8. Considering only the possible positive consequences of an alternative action. Do you feeling guilty or ashamed because you acted one way and wish you had acted in another? Are you looking only at the possibly positive results of the path you didn't take? Are you minimizing that path's possibly negative consequences? When you assess how sound the decisions you made during the assault were, you also must scrutinize the decisions you *didn't* make as thoroughly as those you did (Kubany 1997). This involves brainstorming about how some of the options you didn't choose might have had negative outcomes.

For example, Rachel often wishes she had jumped out of the car while driving to the motel. She thinks that if she had done that, she might have escaped her attacker and avoided the humiliation of others calling her a "wimp" for not even trying to escape. She reasons that, even if she had broken an arm jumping out of the car, it wouldn't have mattered, because the rapist broke her arm anyway.

A more realistic appraisal, however, would require her to consider all the possible negative outcomes of jumping out of a car. For example, she could have sustained injuries far more serious than a broken arm; the car might have gone off the road and struck a pedestrian or another vehicle; and if the rapist had had a gun, he might have tried to shoot her as she fled.

9. Emotional reasoning—using only your emotional reactions as the test of the soundness of your decisions or actions. Emotional reasoning involves judging the merits of a particular action or idea by your emotional reaction to it. Yet feeling a particular way about a particular course of action does not necessarily indicate that pursuing that course of action is in your best interest (Kubany 1997). For example, if you feel guilty about having suffered fewer physical injuries than another survivor, you may feel obligated to listen to her story. Yet the emotional cost of being exposed to her pain might far outweigh any benefit you might give or receive, and listening to her story might even be a disservice to her. If the story retraumatizes you, you may not be able to respond to her in a helpful manner.

Another form of emotional reasoning is mistakenly believing that "feelings are facts," that is, because you *feel* a certain way, you *are* that way; or because a situation feels a certain way, that proves it is that way. For example, "Because I feel guilty, it means

I am guilty." There may be solid reasons for you to feel guilty. However, to verify that your guilt is based on truly guiltworthy actions, more than just feeling guilty is required.

10. All-or-nothing thinking. Life is complex and full of ambiguities. It is, therefore, a serious error to view yourself, others, or life events in oversimplified, absolute terms, for example, to view anyone or any situation as being either all good or all bad, rather than a mix of both. Few life situations are either all-black or all-white. Most are shades of gray (Resick 1994).

11. Exaggerating or minimizing the meaning of an event. The tendency either to exaggerate or minimize the meaning of a negative event is similar to all-or-nothing thinking (Hall and Henderson 1996). It is erroneous for you to think that your assault meant "nothing," and it will not have an impact on your life. It is also erroneous to interpret the assault, as shattering as it was, as the defining moment of your life, or as the core of your identity.

For example, suppose Rachel concluded that because she had ignored her "bad feeling" about going to class, she could no longer trust her judgment in most other matters. As a result of exaggerating the meaning of the assault in this way, she might plunge into a deep depression or decide to quit school. On the other hand, if she minimized the assault by dismissing it as "no big deal," she would be lying to herself. The assault did affect her. Among other ways, it reinforced a fear she had before the assault: that she was not intelligent enough to finish college.

12. Catastrophizing—the only possible outcome will be the worst imaginable one. To catastrophize means concluding that the only possible outcome of a problem situation will be the worst outcome imaginable: that is, a catastrophe. Catastrophic thinking begins with the false assumption that one negative event inevitably leads to an even greater negative event, which automatically leads to a negative event of even greater magnitude, and so on, culminating in a situation where all is lost. The belief that a terrible outcome is inevitable because little can be done to prevent it underlies catastrophic thinking. In most cases, however, some action can be taken to improve matters, and the imagined disastrous ending is only one of many possible outcomes (Freeman and Zaken-Greenberg 1989).

Here's an example of Rachel's catastrophic thinking: "I had two nightmares this week. What will I do if they never stop? I'll never get any sleep so I'll be too tired to study, and I'll flunk out of school. Then, I'll have to take a low-paying job. I'll be so poor, I'll get depressed and won't be able to function at all. I'll even lose my low-paying job. Because I won't be able to pay the rent, I'll become homeless. Then I'll be mugged and raped again. No one will want to be with me, and I'll die all alone. My life is hopeless. So why not give up now?"

As the result of her catastrophic thinking, Rachel was sure that having had two nightmares in one week meant that she would have nightmares forever, and because of that she was doomed to be homeless, loveless, and subject to ongoing abuse. But none of her many conclusions were based on fact. For example, having nightmares after a sexual assault does not automatically lead to decades of troubled sleep, and neither does a single depressive episode lead to a lifelong depression.

Furthermore, Rachel has many options that can keep her from becoming destitute, such as working with self-help books on nightmares and depression, and finding professional help for these problems. While still suffering from post-assault symptoms, she can explore the option of going to school part-time, finding a tutor or a "study buddy," or using her school's educational and counseling support programs.

13. Believing that you and only you were responsible for the assault; that is, ignoring the total number of elements involved and their complex relationships. Women tend to exaggerate the importance of their role during sexual assault. However, women are rarely the sole cause of a devastating event like sexual assault *or any of the negative legal or interpersonal events that may have followed.* Kubany (1997) suggests that individuals in therapy should list all the causative factors involved in a stressful event and then assign a percentage to each factor according to how much they think it contributed to the negative outcome.

Rachel's list of factors contributing to her assault included the following: inadequate security by the campus police; lack of escort services for female students; societal conditions that permit violence against women; the attacker's decision to attack her; all the people alive and dead who contributed to the attacker's distorted notions of masculine power; anyone who might have seen the rapist breaking into her car and done nothing about it; her lack of self-defense skills; and her desire to succeed at school.

By the time Rachel completed her list she had written down more than fifty factors that had contributed to the assault. Her therapist said to her, "You've just laid out all the causes of the assault," and then asked, "If the total percentage is 100, what percentage was your contribution?" Rachel decided that she had made a 12-percent contribution to the assault. Although she still blamed herself, the degree and intensity of her self-blame were considerably reduced by examining the bigger picture.

14. Personalization. Personalization involves concluding that others' decisions and behaviors are directed at you personally when, in fact, they may be motivated by a variety of factors having nothing to do with you. Even if others' actions are motivated by a desire to harm you, that doesn't mean they act solely because of that (Freeman and Zaken-Greenberg 1989). For example, when the judge gave Rachel's attacker a light sentence, Rachel was certain that the judge hadn't liked her and had seen her as a "dumb blonde."

Yet the judge's decision was motivated by the facts that the assailant was a first offender and the local prisons were overcrowded. Also, the judge had recently presided over a rape trial where the victim had been blinded, which made Rachel's injuries seem minor in comparison. On the other hand, Rachel's attorney had devoted himself to her case. Even though she was certain that his efforts were her reward for being a good person, her attorney also wanted to promote his career.

15. Externalization of self-worth. Externalization of self-worth refers to judging yourself by someone else's standards. Women are taught to ground their self-esteem in the approval of others more often than men are. However, the belief that your worth depends on the good opinions of others can lead to low self-esteem, anxiety, shame, and despair. For your self-esteem to be solid and meaningful, it must be based on your values and your view of yourself, not on others' values or view of you (Freeman and Zaken-Greenberg 1989).

Exercise: Looking at the Bigger Picture—A More Rational View

Now, open your journal to page 5, the one you entitled "Thinking Errors," when you were working with chapter 8. The questions in this new exercise will help you to evaluate the rationality of your guilt, shame, and other self-critical emotions. Using these questions as your guide, identify any thinking errors present regarding the thoughts, actions, or emotions you listed on page 3, "Separating Assault-Related Feelings from Other Emotional Issues," of the five pages you created in chapter 8. (You may also want to review your entries for page 2.) Write the name and number of the thinking error on page 5, (entitled "Thinking Errors") and then write two or three sentences about how this thinking error colored your perception of the assault *and any important related events.*

Thinking error 1: Hindsight bias. Are your self-criticisms the result of hindsight bias where you judge what you did, thought, or felt (or didn't do, think, or feel) based on information that was not available to you before or during the assault? Or are your self-criticisms based on omens and premonitions that have no scientific basis? Would you even be thinking of these alleged "signs" if you had never been assaulted?

Thinking error 2: Confusing the possibility that you could have prevented the assault with the belief that you caused it. Do you feel you could've done something that would have averted the assault (or a related negative event)? If you could have prevented this event, then why didn't you? Suppose that you could have prevented it. Does that mean that you caused it by planning it, supporting it, or carrying it out yourself? If you truly believe that you did cause this event, what were your reasons for causing it?

Thinking error 3: Failing to consider or accept this truth: Certain scientifically proven, involuntary, emotional and biological reactions to trauma or extreme stress are so powerful they cannot be controlled by personal determination or willpower.
  Were any of your actions, thoughts, or feelings (or your inability to act, think, or feel) during the assault (or afterward) affected by involuntary biological reactions to trauma or extreme stress, such as the fight or flee, or freeze reactions? (See chapters 2 and 4.) Do you feel humiliated or ashamed because you believe you should have been able to overcome these powerful physiological reactions on the basis of your strength or willpower? Can you accept the scientifically proven fact that it is harder to make good decisions when you are frightened or overwhelmed than when

you feel safe or calm? Do you believe you are exempt from the limitations that affect most people? If so why?

Thinking error 4: Evaluating what you did based on information you discovered *after* the assault, or based on options you thought of *after* the rape. When you assess what you did during your ordeal, are you judging yourself on the basis of information you have now (that you didn't have at the time) or based on options you thought of after the assault? You are not being rational or kind to yourself if you judge the effectiveness or morality of what you did or didn't do based on knowledge you did not have at the time or on ideas you thought of later, after having had time to think about your options and discuss them with others.

Thinking error 5: Judging your actions against improbable options not found in the real world. Are you judging your actions against wished-for or miraculous options that could not possibly exist? Does your guilt or shame reflect your belief that you had superhuman abilities or insights? Do you believe that you are or should have been all-knowing or all-powerful?

Thinking error 6: Catch-22 guilt. Were you in a Catch-22 situation where all the options available to you involved violating a personal standard of right and wrong? Which standard did you violate? Did you betray this standard because of threats or coercion; to protect your life or health or that of others; or to uphold another standard?

Physical survival and psychological integrity are part of the standard of valuing human life. If you acted to protect your physical safety or your self-respect, then you were upholding the value of human life and integrity. Be sure to take into account this standard of self-preservation while you evaluate your decisions and reactions.

Thinking error 7: Judging yourself based on what happened rather than on what you intended to happen. Are your self-criticisms based on what happened rather than what you planned to happen? Are you mistakenly condemning yourself for doing, thinking, or feeling something because of an unforeseen or unintended outcome rather than on the basis of your intentions?

Thinking error 8: Considering only the possible positive consequences of an alternative action. Are you convinced that if you had done something differently during the assault (or a related event), there would have been a better outcome? When you think of what you might have done differently, do you consider only the *possible positive consequences* of this course of action? Have you taken into account any of the *possibly negative consequences* of the alternative actions you wish you had taken?

Thinking error 9: Emotional Reasoning—using only your emotional reactions as the test of the soundness of your decisions or actions. Emotions are important and you need to pay attention to them. However, your emotional reactions cannot be the *only* criteria by which to assess the soundness of your decisions or actions. Are you using your emotions and only your emotions as the measure of the reasonableness of what you did, thought, or felt? Do you have any evidence that supports your self-criticisms other than your emotions?

You could have made the best decisions possible under terrifying circumstances and still felt fear, confusion, guilt, or anger about what you did or did not do. Feeling distressed about what you did may be a sign to you that what you did was wrong. But given the social stigma attached to sexual assault and its intensely personal nature, it's possible you would have negative emotional reactions to your behavior, no matter what you did.

Thinking error 10: All-or-nothing thinking. Do you view people or situations in absolute or extreme terms? For example, do you assume that because some people disapprove of you, most people do? Or because you made a certain error today, you will always make that error in the future? Survivors often struggle with other all-or-nothing thoughts such as "I must do everything perfectly or what I do will be totally worthless" or "My efforts to recover are completely useless because I still have symptoms." Resick (1994) points out that terms or phrases like "always," "forever," "never," "need," "should," "must," "can't," and "every time," signal all-or-nothing thinking.

Thinking error 11: Exaggerating or minimizing the meaning of an event. Are you exaggerating the meaning of the assault by giving it more importance than it really has? Do you believe that the assault has the power to control almost every aspect of your life both now and in the future? Do you believe the assault crippled every part of your life, and that every part of your life will remain as crippled for the rest of your life? On the other hand, you may be minimizing the meaning of the assault. Do you dismiss it as inconsequential or deny its impact on some aspects of your life?

Thinking error 12: Catastrophizing—the only possible outcome will be the worst one imaginable. Do you selectively focus on the most disastrous outcome of a problem? Are you convinced that the only possible outcome to this problem will be catastrophic? Are you ignoring the possibility that positive action can be taken to improve matters?

Thinking error 13: Believing that you and only you were responsible for the assault; that is, ignoring the total number of elements involved and their complex relationships. Do you feel you were the *main* or the *sole* cause of the assault or its negative consequences? Were there any other forces at play? Have you taken on so much responsibility that your attacker (and any others who harmed you) are absolved?

Before you complete page 5, you may need to work on this thinking error on a separate page of your journal. On a new page, write the heading "Causes." Make a list of all the other people and forces involved in causing the assault and its negative repercussions. Include not only the immediate causes, but the more distant ones.

Do not minimize the effects of societal factors such as the huge number of media images linking sex and violence in contrast to the relatively few images linking sex with mutual respect or affection; the plethora of hypersexual images of women; the huge profits of the pornography industry; the violent nature of our society; and the social and economic conditions that breed crime and the sexual exploitation of women.

Did your date, lover, or fiancé threaten to end your relationship or to replace you with another woman if you didn't do what he wanted? Were you made to feel sexually inadequate by being called "uptight," "hung-up," or "frigid"? If these or other forms of psychological coercion were used to pressure you into unwanted sex, then perhaps one of the following factors belongs on your list of causes: social pressures on women to be in a relationship with a man; the greater economic power of men, as compared to women; and current expectations that women should be sexually responsive (in contrast to the not-so-distant past when women were expected to be disinterested in sex). If you tend to see yourself as the central cause of the assault, you may need help in compiling a complete list of causes. If this is the case, you may want to share your list with your therapist, a trusted friend, or a trusted member of your recovery program or group.

After you have generated your list of causes, give each cause a percentage of responsibility (Kubany and Manke 1995). What percentage of the cause belongs to you? How has this exercise altered your original view of your role in the assault?

Thinking error 14: Personalization. Are you assuming that someone's decision or behavior is directed at you personally and that there are no other factors motivating this individual? What evidence do you have to support this belief? Are there any other factors that may be motivating this person?

Suppose that the person whose decision or behavior you think was directed at you personally, was reacting the same way to someone else, say, someone who was higher up. Would you assume that the higher-up person's decisions and behaviors were directed at this other person for personal reasons and that no other motives were possible? What other motives might be possible?

Thinking error 15: Externalization of self-worth. Do you judge the soundness or morality of your actions, thoughts, or behaviors on the basis of others' opinions? That everyone does not understand or approve of what you did (or did not do) is not a sign that you acted like a fool, a wimp, or a "slut." It is almost impossible to receive the approval of most or all people, especially during crises when fear distorts thinking, or during legal proceedings, which are impersonal and adversarial in nature.

How Judy Used Common Thinking Errors

At the end of chapter 8 you were told that Judy grew stronger by learning to recognize some common thinking errors, which helped her to better understand her sexual assault. This section will show you in greater detail how Judy worked with these errors in order to reach new conclusions about her devastating experience. Here's how Judy did this exercise:

She reread what she wrote for each event described on page 1 that resulted in self-critical thoughts and feelings (as she specified on pages 2 and 3). Then she reviewed the various thinking errors described above. She then decided whether her thoughts reflected one or more of these errors. She wrote the names (or numbers) of the thinking errors on page 5. For each error, she wrote at least one sentence, describing how her thoughts illustrated that thinking error and another sentence that put forth a more rational view of the event. Here's an example of Judy's entry for item 4:

Page 1: What Happened?

"I got to the park exactly on time and waited in the car for Peter for an hour."

Page 2: Reactions—Thoughts, Feelings, and Beliefs

"I shouldn't have waited in that car for a whole hour. That made me too restless, and I just had to go take that damned walk. *I should have left right after the park ranger came by*. After he waved at me he turned around and headed for the exit. At the time, I thought that meant everything was safe in the park, so he wasn't needed. But his leaving really *was* a sign that I should go too. But numbskull that I am, I didn't get the message."

Page 4: Assault-Related Negative Thoughts and Feelings

"I feel guilty about being willing to tolerate the emotional and physical stress of waiting in the car that long, because that shows I'm too dependent on Peter, and because the waiting led me to the walk that led to my rape. I also feel guilty for not having realized that when the ranger left the park, that was a sign that I should leave the park."

Page 5: Thinking Errors—Toward a More Rational View

Note that when completing page 5, Judy reviewed the *entire* list of thinking errors. She found, as you probably will, too, that not every thinking error applied to her understanding of each of her entries.

Thinking error no. 1: "It's irrational for me to connect waiting in the car with the assault because I had no knowledge that I might be assaulted. If I had known, I would have left immediately. It's illogical for me to view the ranger's leaving the park as a 'warning sign.' If I hadn't been assaulted, I wouldn't have given his exit a second thought. If a jury of reasonable people were asked if the ranger's exit was an omen foretelling the assault, they would probably disagree. If I had received definitive information that I might be harmed, for example, if the ranger had told me to go home or if there had been a news flash announcing a rapist in the park, I might have cause to feel guilty about not leaving. However, the meaning of the ranger's exit from the park was vague and could be interpreted in a number of various ways."

Thinking error no. 2: "Just because I might have done something to prevent the assault, doesn't mean I caused it. The assailant caused the assault. If I was with someone I knew had a history of sexual assault, then I might be justified in thinking that I contributed to the assault. But that was not the case."

Thinking error no. 9: "Just because I feel stupid for not interpreting the park ranger's leaving as an omen, doesn't mean I am stupid. I can think of hundreds of times I have not acted stupidly. Feeling like I don't have any self-respect doesn't mean that, in fact, I have absolutely no self-respect."

Thinking error no. 10: "It's irrational to think that I don't have any self-respect because I tolerated this discomfort. Self-respect is not an all-or-nothing feeling. By waiting so long in the car, I was not respecting the part of myself that was uncomfortable and felt put-upon. But I was respecting that part of myself which values my relationship with Peter. Even if I displayed no self-respect in this incident, it's unfair and makes no sense to judge my entire self on the basis of this or any other single event."

Thinking error no. 7: "It's irrational for me to feel guilty about taking the walk because my intention in taking the walk was not to act like a slut, but, quite the opposite, to calm myself in preparation for an important discussion."

Page 1: What Happened?

"I thought about poking his eyes with my fingers, but I was afraid this could make him even more brutal. I thought about shoving him too, but all of a sudden I had no strength."

Page 2: Reactions, Thoughts, and Feelings

"Failed again. The one self-defense technique I did finally manage to remember—the eye-poking one—I was too scared to try. Couldn't I have at least tried to shove him off me? He wasn't that big. I thought I was in pretty good shape, but I guess I'm a weakling."

Page 4: Assault-Related Negative Feelings

"I feel guilty I wasn't brave enough to try to poke his eyes out. I feel guilty for not having the strength to shove him off of me. I feel guilty for not taking vitamins, for not exercising more, and for not taking the self-defense class that was offered at the gym a few months ago."

Thinking error no. 2: "Just because I might have prevented the assault by using the eye-poking technique or by shoving the rapist doesn't mean that I caused the assault."

Thinking errors no. 6 and no. 8: "It's illogical for me to feel guilty about not shoving the rapist without considering the possibility that I might not have succeeded, and that he might have retaliated even more violently against me. It's also possible that I might have lost my balance while shoving him, or that he could have shoved me back or grabbed me as he fell. Either way, I could have fallen down those rocks and been seriously hurt, or even killed."

"It's also illogical for me to feel guilty for not having tried to poke the attacker in the eyes without considering the possibility that, if I had tried, I might not have succeeded. Even if I had been an expert at it, under such frightening conditions, I might not have succeeded. Then my attacker might have harmed me more.

"Even if I had succeeded and fled, he might have recovered before I was safely away. Then he could have caught up with me and harmed or killed me, especially, if in my hurry to get away, I twisted my ankle or fell on the rocks and hurt myself."

Thinking error no. 10: "It is illogical to see myself as a weakling or a wimp because it isn't true that I've acted like a wimp or a weakling every single minute of my life. Just as it isn't true that I am always assertive, it isn't true that I'm always nonassertive. Even right after the assault, I was able to assert myself with

Peter when I insisted he take me home instead of to a hospital or to the police!"

Thinking error no. 3: "It is illogical to blame myself for going numb and losing my physical strength, because these were involuntary biological reactions to danger, reactions that can't be overcome by individual strength or willpower."

Getting Feedback

At this point, as at other points in the recovery process, it would be extremely helpful for you to take your writing to your therapist or support group to get some feedback. Others can help point out to you certain realities of the situation or particular strengths that you exhibited that you might have overlooked. (Remember, you have the right to be selective about with whom you share your thoughts and your writing and what you share. Do not allow others, whether peers, therapists, or doctors, to pressure you into sharing if you do not wish to share.) After you have received some feedback, you might want to make some additions to pages 4 and 5.

Exercise 6: Know Your Strengths

Congratulations. You've done quite a lot of work already in completing the exercises in your journal on the pages you numbered 1, 2, 3, 4, and 5. Now, number a fresh page in your journal number 6, and give it the title, "Identifying My Strengths." The last part of this exercise will help you to synthesize all that you have done.

Write at least two sentences about the strengths you exhibited during particular aspects of the assault. For each of the thoughts, actions, or feelings you listed on page 1, identify those about which you feel some pride. Don't worry about seeming vain. Just make a list of all of your positive qualities that you can think of.

You may want to begin as follows: "In this instance I feel proud that I _____ " or "As a result of the way I acted, thought, or felt during those difficult times, I now see myself as _____ ." For example, were you brave, clever, intelligent, resourceful, caring, loyal, moral, emotionally or physically strong, spiritual, focused, or original? If there is anything else positive about what you did, thought, or felt (or didn't do, think, or feel), be sure to list that on page 6 as well. For example, here's what Judy's wrote about two of her strengths:

Item 4: "In this instance, I displayed self-control, patience, and loyalty to my commitment to Peter. That I was able to be uncomfortable for so long without biting my nails or cursing shows that I have made progress in mastering two of my bad habits."

Item 11: "Refraining from using a self-defense technique I hadn't mastered, in a situation where I might have been injured anyway, shows that I have good instincts."

After completing this exercise, Judy realized that if her relationship with Peter was going to last, it would have to change and become an equal partnership. As important as he had been to her in the past, he was no longer the center of her life. Cherishing herself had become more important to her than pleasing him (or anyone else for that matter).

CHAPTER 10

Healing Exercises

Congratulations. If you've completed all the exercises in this book thus far, you've done a huge amount of work. It's very likely that during the painstaking process of repeatedly reviewing the assault, you experienced many painful feelings. Confronting these feelings is an act of immense courage, since the usual tendency is to avoid them at all costs.

Coping with Self-Critical Thoughts and Feelings

Despite all that you have learned, when you think of events related to your assault, your first response still may be to feel as frightened, anxious, numb, guilty, or helpless as you did before your recovery efforts. Do not be dismayed. If you have spent months or years thinking about the assault irrationally, you cannot expect to begin thinking more rationally immediately. Your old point of view will dominate for a while.

It's fine to have others point out your distorted beliefs about what happened. You may always need this kind of support; there is no shame in needing ongoing help. It is also important, however, for you to be able to correct your thinking on your own. In the final analysis, the ultimate battle for recovery takes place inside your head. To win this battle, you need to reprogram your mind to think more rationally.

The first challenge is to learn to catch yourself when you start berating yourself for something you did or didn't do, something you felt or didn't feel, or something you thought or didn't think. The second challenge is to counter these accusations by reminding yourself about the various kinds of thinking errors and about what you have learned about sexual assault. This is not easy to do. However, if you can observe yourself thinking irrationally even one time, it will be easier to do the second time, then the third time, and so on, until eventually it becomes a habit.

Even if thinking rationally about what happened does not become a habit and you always have to work hard to orient yourself toward a more hopeful view of life and yourself, that doesn't mean you're a failure. It simply means you were *severely* traumatized, and that, therefore, it will be even harder for you to undo the damage inflicted on you. But, contrary to any twisted notions about your identity that your attacker or others may have etched on your psyche, you are worth the effort.

Your goal is to become increasingly able to catch yourself when you fall into your old irrational ways of thought, and be able to say to yourself, "Wait a minute. Haven't I already figured out that I can look at this differently? I don't need to feel _____ about _____ the way I used to." You will need to practice countering your old illogical self-criticisms with more realistic statements over and over again, until thinking logically becomes as automatic as condemning yourself for illogical reasons.

Are you already feeling overwhelmed at the thought of all the practice involved in correcting your point of view? If so, consider how much time and emotional energy were wasted by the thoughts and feelings you used to have. In the long run, it's faster, easier, and perhaps less expensive (in terms of doctor's visits, lost productivity, missed opportunities, etc.) to take the time to retrain your mind than to not make the effort to benefit from all the hard work you already have invested in working with this book.

Exercise: Practicing Rational Thinking

In this exercise you will learn to counter your irrational thoughts about the assault by writing them down in a more rational way and, then, speaking these more rational views aloud. At first, talking out loud to yourself may seem very weird, but is it a powerful way to help yourself heal. Begin by reading the following paragraph several times, until you thoroughly understand it and you know what you will need to write to fill in the blanks. Then fill in the blanks for any irrational thoughts about the assault that still trouble you—one irrational thought at a time. Afterward read, reread, and say the contents of this paragraph over and over again, until they are memorized.

"When I was assaulted, _____ happened. Whenever I remember this, I usually think _____ and I feel (anxious, numb, guilty, powerless, ashamed, depressed, hopeless). When I start feeling _____ about _____ , I need to remind myself that I'm thinking incorrectly. Instead of practicing the thinking error that [insert a description of the relevant thinking error], I need to look at it this way: [insert rational thought]. I also need to remember that I displayed the following strengths [list strengths] and I need to give myself credit for these. Just as it would be a mistake for me to concentrate on all the good things in life to the exclusion of the things I feel _____ about, so, too, would it be a mistake to focus entirely on the negative and exclude the positive."

You can further strengthen your new way of thinking by standing in front of a mirror and watching yourself as you speak your more rational thoughts out loud; by saying them to trusted others; or by recording them on audiotape. Another possibility would be to form a vision of yourself as you hope to be in the future: include not only what you hope to be doing, but how you hope to be feeling. You could make a poster or collage of this vision of yourself with words and pictures cut from magazines, your own artwork, and other materials. When you look at it, let its meaning penetrate.

Exercise: Silencing the Inner Critic

"This will never work, . . . it's ridiculous, too simple, too embarrassing," you may be thinking as you speak your rational thoughts aloud. This is the voice of your inner critic. Now that you are so close to the finish line, it is predictable that this critic will emerge to remind you that you don't deserve to feel better about yourself or that you are too damaged to be healed (Cameron 1992).

Are you ashamed of your inner critic's messages? Do you try to mask them from others? From yourself? Perhaps like many women today, you feel it is not acceptable for women to put themselves down. However, it is crucial that you take a good hard look at these nasty messages: they are the sledgehammers with which you have been bludgeoning yourself. If you don't know what your inner critic is saying, then you can't fight back, and you must fight back.

You need to challenge your inner critic's scathing judgments of you with positive affirmations about yourself. In this exercise you will identify as many of your inner critic's barbs as you can, then convert each one into a positive affirmation. When your inner critic rears its ugly head, you can counter its demoralizing messages with one of these affirmations.

Affirmations are not magical cures. To have long-lasting effects, they need to be grounded in the intense kind of emotional work and intellectual analysis that you have completed thus far by working with this book. During this transition period when you are trying to regain your faith in yourself, affirmations (no matter how simplistic they may sound) can help you to refute and ultimately to silence your inner critic.

The most effective affirmations are those that refer to your inherent value as a person, to one of your strengths, or to your potential to develop a particular positive quality, rather than to others' reactions. For example, suppose your inner critic whines, "You're too stupid to recover." To respond, "My teachers don't think I'm stupid," relies on others' reactions. Within seconds, your inner critic is likely to discredit your teachers and begin reeling off examples of the times you acted like a fool.

Your inner critic can also undermine affirmations containing lies or fantastic claims like, "I got all A's in school without ever studying." It will be much harder for your inner critic to attack truths that don't require "evidence" but come from your heart—truths like this: Like all human beings, you deserve dignity and respect and are capable of positive change. With this approach, you could respond to the "You are stupid" allegation with affirmations like, "I'm willing to learn," or "I deserve to treat myself with dignity."

On a new page in your journal called "Silencing My Inner Critic," draw a line down the middle of the page. Label the left side "My Inner Critic's Accusations" and the right side "Affirmations of My Worth and Power." Write as many of the negative messages as you can remember on the left side. For each accusation, create and write an affirmation on the right side of the page.

Here are some samples:

Inner Critic's Message	Affirmation of My Worth and Power
Women who are raped deserve punishment.	I deserve to be happy.
You're so _____ , nothing can help you.	I deserve to be healed.
You'll never enjoy sex again.	I deserve to be a woman.
No one will ever like you.	I am a lovable person.
People think you're a _____ .	What others think of me is not my business.
These affirmations will never work.	What I do matters.

Giving your inner critic a name is another way to silence it. You can name it after the man who attacked you, someone else who hurt you, or a negative quality. By calling your inner critic "Ugly," "Stupid," or by any name other than yours, you can begin to view it as an entity apart from you, rather than as a part of your being. Suppose you name your critic "Tim." When Tim begins to criticize you, say (aloud or to yourself), "I'm busy, Tim. Go away"; "Tim, you bore me"; or "Tim, you make no sense. Get lost!"

You can also begin to detach from your inner critic by forming a mental image of it as any person, color, animal, or entity you want it to be, as long as you depict yourself as more powerful. For example, you could picture your inner critic as a midget or as someone wearing a dunce cap or a big sign that says "Liar." Some survivors have delighted in depicting their inner critic as their attacker in a disempowered or humiliating state, such as wearing diapers, sucking his thumb, or sitting behind bars.

You can also imagine yourself involved in an enjoyable or necessary activity while the inner critic is harassing you. Yet in spite of the critic's bothersome presence, you continue focusing on what you need or want to do. You can make this image even more powerful if you can envision the inner critic's voice becoming progressively dimmer until it is barely audible. Visualizing violence is not recommended.

Self-Forgiveness

Forgiving yourself means that you give up the right to blame yourself for what you could not control. You may have achieved some level of intellectual self-forgiveness through your rational analysis of the assault. However, emotional self-forgiveness can take much longer and it requires you to acknowledge and process your anger, grief, and other strong feelings. Sometimes it helps to remember that your attacker was an emotionally disturbed person whose cruelty had little to do with you. (This does not mean that you have to forgive the attacker.) Your first step to emotional self-forgiveness is to identify the actions, thoughts, or emotions for which you feel the need to forgive yourself.

Exercise: Self-Forgiveness

On a new page in your journal entitled "Self-Forgiveness," answer the following questions: For which aspects of the assault do you still blame yourself? What would it take for you to forgive yourself for these reactions? Is it possible for you to do whatever you described above so that you can forgive yourself? If so, what prevents you from doing so?

Coping with Anger and Rage

Sometimes survivors turn their anger at the offender (or others who harmed them) into guilt and shame. In some instances, a woman may carry so much guilt and shame that it can seem as if her assailant is exonerated. This often occurs when others "excuse" the offender or when he hasn't been brought to justice.

In her work with Holocaust survivors, Yael Daniele (1998) found that, for these victims, feeling guilty helped them to maintain their belief in a just world. In the case of sexual assault, the same construct may hold true. A survivor can make sure that at least one person in the world suffers remorse for what happened, even if that person happens to be herself.

The following exercise may help you take the condemnation that belongs to the offender off your shoulders and onto his, where it rightfully belongs.

Exercise: Identifying Shame and Guilt Belonging to the Attacker

On a new page in your journal entitled "Shame and Guilt Belonging to My Attacker," answer the following questions: About what actions, thoughts, and feelings should my attacker feel guilty or ashamed? According to the law, for what actions should he be punished? According to my religion or spiritual beliefs, for what actions, thoughts, or feelings does he need to seek correction and ask forgiveness? If you wish, you can also complete this exercise for those individuals and institutions who discounted your pain or disrespected you. Begin with one person or agency. Later on, you can return and, if you feel it is necessary, complete this exercise with another individual or agency.

Exercise: Letter to the Attacker

On a new page in your journal called "Letter to My Offender," write a letter to your attacker telling him how the assault has affected your life. Since this letter is for you and only you, you don't have to be nice. However, the moment your anger begins to feel out of control, STOP. You may want to read this letter to your therapist.

Do not, under any circumstances, read or mail this letter to the assailant, to the police, to members of the legal system (including your attorney), or to anyone who isn't legally bound to maintain your confidentiality. In the wrong hands, such a letter could be construed as harassment or as a threat, and you might come under legal scrutiny. Even helping professionals are legally mandated to report persons whom they suspect might harm another person. Destroy the letter soon you have written it. If you wish, you can write similar letters to persons and organizations who harmed you. Keep these letters confidential also and destroy them promptly.

Commemorating Your Losses

Public memorials, such as funerals, serve important healing functions. They legitimize loss and communicate the message that "This terrible event happened and it happened to me. It hurt then and it hurts now. My sorrow deserves to be respected." There are numerous memorials for war veterans. But there are no monuments or memorial services for survivors of sexual assault. Survivors of national traumas, such as the September 11th attacks, do not have to bear their pain alone. Not only their family members and friends, but their entire community share their pain. In contrast, sexual assault survivors are expected to keep their grief a secret and to shoulder their pain alone, without community support, save for a few select professionals.

You have every right to be angry, if not furious, at this lack of public recognition and validation for your suffering. However, just because society does not acknowledge your losses, doesn't mean that you can't do so. The following suggestions are offered as possible ways to commemorate your assault.

Commemorating Your Pain and Grief

Around the anniversary of the assault, or at other times when you feel the need to honor your past, you can do one or all of the following:

1. Ask someone to be with you for all or part of the day. You need not talk about the assault. You might simply ask her or him to have a meal with you, take a walk, watch a video, or listen to music together.

2. Make a charitable donation or provide a service to the needy or an organization that helps sexual assault survivors.

3. Make a drawing, a sculpture, or a music tape that reflects your feelings or simply write about your feelings.

4. Set aside time to read poems or other literature written by survivors, or other reading matter about loss, hope, or any topic that, in your view, recognizes and honors your experience. There is a vast amount of literature concerned with the themes of injustice and loss. Ask your librarian for assistance. Once again, be sure to monitor your reactions and stop reading if you become overly distressed.

5. Honor your losses by creating a ritual, planting a tree or a plant, or buying yourself a flower.

6. Treat your traumatized self gently and give her something nurturing and comforting, be it just a cup of tea. Don't pretend she isn't there and don't tell her that she needs to "get over it," or that you never want to see her again.

7. Repeat to yourself, "I can live in the present while also honoring the past."

8. At the very least, take a moment of silence, if not for yourself, then for the millions of other sexual assault survivors in this world.

You can ask other survivors how they commemorate their losses or discuss possibilities with your therapist and trusted others. Although you can commemorate your assault privately, you might also find comfort by including at least one other person.

Exercise: Turning Anger into Change

The anger borne from unjust suffering runs deep. You are entitled to your fury, but you are not entitled to express your anger by harming yourself or others. Julia Cameron wrote that "Anger is meant to be acted upon. It is not meant to be acted out" (1992, 62). As summarized by the logo of the DC Rape Crisis Center, "Turning Anger into Change," the purpose of recovery is not to remove your anger, but to find ways to channel it toward a constructive goal. If you are angry about the assault until the day you die, that is fine. However, if your anger comes to dominate your inner being or damage areas of your life that you hold precious, then the assailant has harmed you again. Finding constructive outlets for your justifiable rage can help to prevent the assault from taking over more of your life than it already has.

On a new page in your journal entitled "Turning Anger into Change," write four or five sentences about how you might turn your anger into change. If you are angry about being angry, because you resent the intrusion of this anger into your life, or because you have the burden of having to manage your anger, write about these matters too.

Making Amends

Perhaps there were times when you misdirected your anger regarding the assault onto people who did not deserve it. If you feel guilty about these actions, you may want to apologize or make amends to these people. Consult appendix B for relevant readings, especially the books on relationships and the literature on twelve-step programs and addiction.

Therapeutic Approaches and Professional Assistance

In recent years innovative techniques, such as EMDR (eye movement desensitization and reprocessing) and energy tapping, have been developed to help the survivors of extremely stressful traumas such as sexual assault. You can find out more about these techniques from a qualified mental health professional, a local mental health agency or organization, or by consulting appendix B, which also lists self-help books on eye movement therapy and energy tapping.

If you should decide to try out EMDR, energy tapping therapy, or any other type of technique, keep in mind that these are techniques and, like any techniques, they should be part of a comprehensive therapy program conducted by a therapist who is familiar with you and qualified in the area of sexual assault. In addition, because each person is unique, no single technique can be guaranteed to help everyone.

Spirituality

Note: This brief section on spirituality is not intended to be a spiritual guide or to promote any particular spiritual, religious, or existential orientation or practice. It is offered as a stepping-stone for those survivors who wish to examine the impact of the assault on their spiritual or religious beliefs. However, to be mentally healthy or to recover, it is by no means necessary to be interested in or deal with spiritual or religious matters. If such issues do not concern you, skip this section and proceed to the "Checking In" section at the end of this chapter.

Sexual assault may have enhanced your spirituality, or it may have eroded it. You may feel that your faith or your beliefs betrayed you, or the opposite—that you betrayed them. If you are like many survivors, you ricochet back and forth between these two points of view.

You may also have met some form of spiritual "blame-the-victim" belief system where the assault (or its negative effects) are viewed in one of the following ways: as a form of "payback" or punishment for your wrongdoings; as a divinely ordained means of emotional or spiritual development; as the result of your anger at your attacker or at others who have harmed you; or as the result of some form of spiritual inadequacy, for example, not praying enough or in the right way, not attending services, or not having adequately forgiven those who have harmed you.

Although you may be discouraged and dismayed by such attitudes, you still may want a spiritual explanation for your assault to help you salvage your strengths and provide you with spiritual direction. But you may be confused about how to proceed. One way to begin is for you to clarify your spiritual or religious beliefs. The following exercise can help you explore your spirituality and examine how it has been affected by your assault.

Exercise: Taking Stock—Spiritual Issues

1. Write a spiritual autobiography: Describe your spiritual beliefs and experiences throughout your life. What key experiences influenced your spiritual beliefs and your sense of purpose in life? Describe the impact of the assault on your sense of purpose.

2. Answer the following questions: Where do you stand on the issues of good and evil in the world? On the issue of the suffering of the innocent? On your feelings of anger at being betrayed or abandoned by the universe? Did the

assault confirm the views you had before it took place, or did it change your views? If so, how?

3. Attend a religious or spiritual service or meet with a spiritual or religious leader of your choice. Afterward, think about this experience, write about it, and talk about it in order to clarify your personal beliefs and identify sources of confusion, certainty, or hope.

Checking in: Return to the "Directions for Checking In" at the end of chapter 1 and answer all the questions to the best of your ability.

CHAPTER 11

Victories, Strengths, and Hopes

You've reached the last chapter of this book. What a victory! Despite the emotionally wrenching nature of the healing process, you've persisted in your efforts. You've learned coping skills and rational ways of thinking that will help you with the remainder of your recovery, as well as with future life stresses.

Assessing Your Progress

Now it is time to take stock of your progress and savor it. It is also time to reflect on what you might have learned as the result of all your agony.

Exercise: Assessing Your Progress

In chapter 7, you examined the effects of the assault on various aspects of your life. Now you will examine the impact of the assault once more, this time in terms of your present perspective. Label a new page in your journal "Assessing My Progress" and divide it into three columns. Label the first column "Aspect of

Life," the second "Prerecovery Assessment of Effects," and the third "Updated Assessment of Effects." Return to your journal entry for Exercise 3: "My Life—Before and after the Assault" in chapter 7. In column 1, copy the list of the various aspects of life as described in Exercise 3. In column 2, copy the journal entries you made for each aspect of your life in Exercise 3. Now answer the questions in Exercise 3 in terms of your current perceptions. Write these answers in column 3.

Compare your entries in column 2 with those in column 3. Do you notice any improvements? On a new page in your journal entitled "My Progress," write all of these positive changes, no matter how small. Can you take credit for these gains and reward yourself accordingly? Even if you were greatly helped by others, it was you who had the humility, self-love, and courage to find that help and use it to help yourself heal.

Now, on a new page in your journal entitled "Areas That Need Healing," make a list of the areas of that still need healing. Don't expect the negative effects of the assault to have lessened in every area. Some of the physical and financial consequences of the assault may be difficult, if not impossible, to reverse. Some relationship problems also may be long lasting, especially if the other person involved is making no effort to communicate. In the exercise "Action Plans" below, you will begin thinking about what steps you might take to improve those areas still needing healing, provided they are realistically capable of being changed.

Still Reacting to Triggers

If, when you encounter a trigger, you experience anxiety, depression, increased nightmares, or other symptoms, this doesn't mean you have not recovered. As previously explained, human beings are biologically programmed to respond to situations of great danger with the fight, flight, or freeze reactions. When they encounter reminders of their frightening experience, they may react similarly and find themselves experiencing one or more of common trigger reactions. (See chapter 4 for descriptions of fight, flight, and freeze responses, common triggers, and common trigger reactions.)

Major life changes, whether negative or positive, and expected life transitions, such as graduation or marriage, also can resurrect old distressing memories. This doesn't mean you haven't made much progress: it simply means that whenever there is a major change in your life, your psyche needs to reorganize its understanding of the assault and its role in your life.

It bears repeating that trigger reactions are involuntary. Therefore it is impossible to define recovery as never again remembering the assault or never again having a trigger reaction. Instead, as Harvey (1996) explains, recovery must be assessed using measures like these: improved self-care; increased acceptance of trigger reactions; increased willingness to try to manage trigger reactions constructively; and increased involvement in present-day life.

Exercise: Standards of Recovery

On a new page in your journal entitled "Personal Growth," answer the following questions: Are you increasingly able to accept your feelings, especially uncomfortable ones like anger and shame? Are you increasingly able to experience these and other negative emotions, without trying to mask them with an addiction or other negative behavior? Are you taking action to help yourself heal from your grief, shame, guilt, self-doubts, and other painful feelings? Are you trying to find constructive outlets for your anger?

Have you honored the contract you made in chapter 2 regarding your physical safety? Have you sought professional help for any symptoms of depression, post-traumatic stress disorder, an addiction, or any other distressing problem? Are you increasingly able to accept, or to manage, any of your symptoms? Are you increasingly able to counter your irrational thoughts with more rational ones?

Have you honored the contract you made in chapter 3 regarding your support system? Are you careful to share your innermost thoughts and feelings only with those who are safe? Are you experiencing more joy and love in your life?

Answering yes to *any* of the questions above indicates that you are making progress. If you haven't rewarded yourself for your progress, do so now.

Looking Forward

Recovery involves more than looking backward. It also involves looking forward toward finding realistic ways to take the best care of yourself as possible and, within the limitations of your life circumstances, toward finding ways of shaping your life so it reflects your priorities and the longings of your heart.

Exercise: Action Plans

On a new page in your journal entitled "Action Plans," write down the concerns listed in your journal entry "Areas That Need Healing" from this chapter. For each concern, write what you might be able to do to help yourself. In some areas, the damage may be permanent or may require financial or other resources not available to you. If these or other conditions make it extremely difficult or impossible to improve matters, write that down, too.

Ask your therapist, support group, or trusted others for suggestions. You may also want to consult with specialists in areas where you experience ongoing distress, such as headaches, allergies, sexual dysfunction, or anxiety. Even if you are satisfied with the professional care you are receiving, a second opinion for medical or psychological concerns might result in insights that could be useful to your current provider.

Do not try to implement all of your action plans at the same time. Start with one, perhaps the one where positive change matters the most to you.

The Limitations of Recovery and Therapy

While working with this book, you may have felt frustrated with it or with your other recovery efforts, perhaps more so now that you are almost at the finish line. Your frustration may have turned to anger as you realized that all the insights and coping skills in the world cannot erase the assault or make your life today pain or anxiety-free.

Unfortunately, some mental health professionals, self-help books, and media presentations foster the unrealistic notion that therapy is a cure-all. They promote the myth that if you adhere to the "rules," or psychologically sound principles for living, then you can develop ironclad self-confidence, eternal optimism, and nearly total freedom from your past.

When people who have followed a program outlined by a mental health professional or a self-help book find that they are still distressed, they are often told that their suffering will ease if only they try harder, "let go," "think positive," "take charge," or inflict a "tough love" policy on themselves or others. This is false advertising, for no amount of personal growth can guarantee such ironclad self-confidence, eternal optimism, or nearly total freedom from your past.

Like psychotherapy, recovery can help you to be more honest and compassionate with yourself and help you to better understand and cope with your emotions and the impact of your past experiences. It can also help you perceive and pursue more options for your life, but it is not an entry ticket to your life dreams.

Recovery from sexual assault cannot eliminate problems you had prior to the assault, which may need some attention. Neither can recovery, or any form of inner personal growth, protect you from the impact of external realities like sociopolitical trends, economic changes, illness and death in the family, and the passage of time. Unfortunately, there are some problems that have no solutions.

The skills and perspectives you have learned in recovery can help you to cope better with external realities. However, they cannot spare you from the inevitable struggles and misfortunes involved in human existence.

Exercise: Frustrations with the Limits of Recovery and Therapy

On a new page in your journal entitled "Frustrations with the Limits of Recovery and Therapy," write at least two or three sentences in response to the following questions: What problems do you have now that you had hoped would be alleviated by recovery or therapy, but which you now realize cannot be significantly improved by such efforts?

Suppose you had never been in recovery or therapy. How would your view of and approach toward these ongoing problems be different? Has being in recovery helped at all with these problems? If so, how? In what ways has being in recovery provided little or no help with these problems? How do you feel about the fact that your increased self-awareness and your coping skills have only limited power to alleviate these problems?

Exercise: What Have You Learned?

According to ancient sages from many cultures and brilliant writers throughout the centuries, wisdom can be born only from sorrow. Dostoyevsky in *Notes from the Underground* wrote "Suffering is the sole origin of consciousness." You have learned the truth of this remark as the result of your personal encounter with human cruelty.

On a new page in your journal entitled "What I Have Learned," write at least three sentences in response to the following questions: What have you learned about yourself, about others, or about life in general as the result of experiencing the torture of sexual assault; the stress of having to cope with the disruptions it inflicted on your life; and the challenges of the healing process?

How could you use what you've learned if life confronts you with another violent or unjust situation or another major loss? If you want to help others, how could you use what you've learned to benefit other victims of sexual assault or of other tragic events?

The person who attacked you could have killed you. Has coming so close to your own death brought you any closer to living your life according to your values and needs as opposed to the values and needs of others? If so, in what ways? If not, why not?

Has the grim realization that a single act of human malice could have robbed you of your life or health resulted in you taking your wishes, needs, and talents more seriously? If so, in what ways? If not, why not?

Checking in: Return to the "Directions for Checking In" at the end of chapter 1 and answer all the questions to the best of your ability.

EPILOGUE

It Almost Happened to Me

One Sunday morning while I was working on this book, a man slipped into my home. I had just come back from the gym, taken off my coat, and turned to shut the door —only to find a man standing in my hallway. He asked, "Can I come in?" He had a childish face, a timid demeanor, and from the religious pamphlets he was carrying, he appeared to be a missionary of some kind.

But I sensed danger. I slammed the door and yelled at him to go away. I had to yell several times. He finally left. I was calling the police when I looked outside a window and saw him running from one neighbor's backyard to another, peering over their fences. Then, for some reason, he ran away.

I called the police and was referred to their nonemergency line. It took more than a half hour to get through. The woman who answered the phone asked me several times why hadn't I called sooner, in an accusatory tone implying that I was lying. Then she curtly informed me that because the man was no longer in sight, and I couldn't tell her on what street he might be running, the police would not be dispatched. "Call us when you see him again," she said and hung up the phone.

I alerted a few more neighbors and then I went to church and the grocery store. As usual, I left my backdoor open to carry in my groceries. Within minutes, the man who had come to my door earlier that morning walked into my kitchen. The minute I saw him there, I started to scream loudly and repeatedly. I didn't decide to scream. The screams just started coming out, each one louder than the last. He turned around and left. Even after he fled, I kept on screaming. I couldn't make myself stop, even though I had to call the police.

They came in minutes, were exceptionally supportive, and were quite upset at not having been informed about my earlier call. Had they known a man of this description was in the area, they'd have come out immediately. They had been looking for him for quite some time. According to the police, a man matching my intruder's description had raped several women in my neighborhood.

That evening I tried to continue working on this book, but I couldn't stop shaking. That lasted for some days. For several weeks, I had nausea, nightmares, flashbacks, backaches, and was "hyper"—my whole body was on emergency alert. Anytime there was a knock at the door, even if I was expecting someone, I'd start screaming.

My senses were so acute I could hear a plastic bag rustling in another room. I investigated every slight noise for possible danger. I slept with the lights on in every room and woke up two or three times a night to double-check that the doors were locked. Now, I am committed to keeping an alarm system on at all times, and I follow the police's suggestion of carrying pepper spray with me at all times, even during daylight hours.

Without the coping techniques described in this book, I probably wouldn't have been able to function at all. As it was, five minutes after reading something, I could scarcely remember what I had read. I paid my bills with blank checks and stashed my car keys in the freezer. I spent time searching for "lost" manuscript pages, only to find them right in my hands.

I became afraid not only of the intruder, but also of myself. In addition to memory and concentration problems, I became overreactive and irritable. I worried about what would happen if I wasn't able to control my reactions all the time. What if I ended up snapping at a client? I was grateful for having coping skills, but I bitterly resented the time and energy it took to manage myself just to appear to be normal.

I once had my head beaten into the sidewalk by a mugger and I've been physically assaulted in other ways. But none of these experiences left me with the burning shame I felt after the intrusion and possible assault—because this incident had a sexual innuendo.

Despite all that I knew about sexual assault, I could not erase the effect of centuries of women being made to feel ashamed of their sexuality and responsible for the attacks perpetrated upon them. I knew this feeling was ridiculous, especially since I hadn't been assaulted—only frightened, but somewhere deep within my core, I felt ashamed of being a natural, sexual woman.

I knew better than to tell certain people about the incident. Either my account would fall on deaf ears because they never liked to hear about anything unpleasant, or if they did listen, they would try to find some way to blame me. Yet even when I shared my story with people I trusted, I would wonder if they were thinking that I had "provoked" the incident because I wore makeup, liked to dance, dated sometimes—or I had left my back door unlocked. How careless of me!

However, as a result of working with the exercises in this book, I realized that if the door hadn't been unlocked, the man might have found another more violent way to enter my home. I also realized that the intruder's mental problems and whatever had prevented the police from coming out the first time they were called were far more important than anything I had done—or not done.

For weeks I was barraged with illogical ideas like, "If only you hadn't been rushing to unload the groceries so you could get back to your writing, you would have noticed that he was waiting for you." Or, "Remember three years ago when you forgot to pull the shades when you were undressing. He probably saw you then and he thought that 'you were asking for it.'" Eventually, the methods provided in this book helped me to correct my thinking and freed my mental energy for other matters.

I wasn't harmed. I wasn't even touched, and still I had all these psychological and physiological reactions. I shudder to think of what it must be like to *actually* be sexually violated. To those of you who have suffered the full reality of sexual assault, my heart goes out to you. It is now clearer to me than ever before, that any woman, regardless of her age, social status, looks, or personality, can become a victim of sexual assault, at any time, at any place.

I am also convinced that healing is possible—that the psychological consequences of sexual assault can be managed and need not devastate a woman's life forever. I know that if a woman is able to access wise, compassionate guidance and counseling she will be able to heal even after suffering the most devastating sexual assault.

Dr. Matsakis offers lectures for the public and professional training on trauma-related issues but, regretfully, cannot reply to individual phone calls and letters. For assistance, please contact one of the resources listed in appendix A.

Getting Help—Survivors Groups and Therapy Programs

Anyone who has been sexually assaulted can benefit from the right kind of help. Notice, however, the phrase "the right kind." If the assault damaged your self-esteem, you may need to convince yourself that you deserve a therapy program, whether individual or group, that offers quality sexual assault counseling and that is suited to your individual needs. The subject of this appendix is finding and evaluating therapists, treatment programs, and survivors groups.

Minimum Criteria for Effective Sexual Assault Counseling

Unfortunately, there are many therapists and programs that should be avoided. For example, in recent years, sexual assault and incest have received a great deal of media attention. As a result, some therapists and program directors jumped on that bandwagon. Although they claim to be qualified to treat sexual trauma, the only training they may have is a few workshops and, perhaps, some extremely limited experience. You cannot assume that even a licensed social worker, psychologist, or psychiatrist has had adequate training in sexual assault. As of this writing, such training is not required to obtain a degree in any mental health field.

Nevertheless, there is a minimum set of criteria for effective sexual assault counseling. The only therapists or recovery programs you should consider must do the following:

- Regard your account of your sexual assault as real and important in itself, apart from your other concerns. View you as capable of being healed. Not view you as a willing participant in the assault, nor as someone genetically or biochemically addicted to abuse, nor as a hopeless psychiatric case or addict.

- Be familiar with and able to educate you about the facts of sexual assault; the grieving process; the various kinds of post-assault reactions, such as depression, post-traumatic stress disorder, and dissociation; the physical, sexual, and interpersonal aftereffects of sexual trauma; the nature of the recovery process; and the faulty thinking patterns that can lead to an irrational sense of unworthiness, guilt, shame, powerlessness, and hopelessness.

- Be aware of the effects of racism, sex-role stereotyping and blame-the-victim attitudes on the recovery process and not evidence such biases themselves.

- Provide you with information about assault-related health and legal issues or be willing to get this information for you or direct you to sources where you can obtain it for yourself.

- Be willing to listen to details of the assault yet not pressure you to share aspects of the assault that you do not wish to disclose.

- Be willing not to push you to discuss the assault if you are coping with a current life crisis; if you have an untreated addiction, psychiatric, or medical problem; or if you develop any of the warning signs listed in the "Cautions" section of the introduction to this book.

- Teach you coping skills, such as relaxation techniques or anger management, or make appropriate referrals for you to receive such help.

- Use or recommend medication and behavior-management techniques when appropriate, but not to the exclusion of examining the assault or any past and present events important to you.

Finding a Therapist

In choosing a therapist or treatment program, you have the right to shop around and ask questions. To begin the selection process compile a list of names. Get recommendations from friends, doctors, and people who report having had positive therapeutic experiences; from hospitals with specialized treatment programs for survivors of trauma, especially for sexual trauma, child abuse, or incest; the police; university health or counseling centers (if you are a student); and local mental health and social services agencies, which are usually run by your city or the county.

Local addiction and eating disorders treatment programs, local battered women's and sexual assault centers and hot lines, local women's health centers, and other local women's organizations usually have referral lists of trauma specialists. Local chapters of the Anxiety Disorders Association of America, the International Society for Traumatic Stress Studies, the American Psychiatric Association, the American Psychological Association, the National Association of Social Workers, and the National Organization for Women (NOW) also may have lists of qualified professionals. If you are or were in the military, contact your local military or veterans' hospital or outreach center to inquire about their sexual trauma programs.

Your telephone directory, local library, or social service agency can provide you with the phone numbers of the organizations listed here. If you contact any of these organizations, be sure to inquire if the therapist and programs are identified by specialty, such as sexual trauma or depression. Contact only those therapists whose specialty areas match your needs.

The Screening Process

When you have obtained the names of at least four or five therapists who seem to meet the minimum criteria for effective sexual assault counseling listed above and whose specialties seem to fit your needs, call and interview each of them by phone. (If you are considering a program, you will interview a program representative or staff member.) Before inquiring about qualifications, ask about available openings and fees, including the possibility of a sliding scale. Eliminate therapists and programs that are geographically inaccessible, whose fees are prohibitive, and whose available time slots do not work for you.

If the therapist or program meets your needs in these areas, then inquire about their training, experience, and focus. You must inquire about these matters to verify that any potential therapist or program does, in fact, meet the criteria listed above for effective sexual assault counseling. Do not be afraid to ask how many workshops the therapist or staff members have attended; how many books they have read about sexual assault or related topics, especially women's health issues, depression, post-traumatic stress syndrome (PTSD), or addiction; how they keep up with the latest developments in the area of sexual assault and related areas; and whether they have colleagues available for consultation who are experts in areas relevant to your recovery.

You needn't sound hostile, but don't avoid asking the hard questions for fear of offending. Remember, your mental and physical health are at stake. You can preface your questions by stating that you are faced with a bewildering array of alternatives and you want to make the best choice for yourself.

Consider asking questions such as the following (if you are considering a program, you would ask these questions in terms of the program's staff):

How long have you been in practice? Are you a member of any professional organizations? How many sexual assault survivors have you treated? What is your formal training in the areas of (a) sexual assault, (b) stress and trauma, and (c) depression and addictions? What, in your view, constitutes the recovery process? What approaches would you take toward helping with some of the secondary problems arising from sexual assault, such as substance abuse, eating disorders, dissociation, or depression? What would you do if I became suicidal or felt out of control?

If you receive satisfactory answers to those questions, then ask these: What is your view on self-help groups or other group therapies? If you want couples or family counseling, ask these questions: Do you conduct couples or family therapy? If not, do you work with colleagues who do? Is there a charge for phone calls or other services provided outside of scheduled sessions?

After you have narrowed your list down to two or three therapists or programs, visit them. Most therapists charge full fee for an initial visit. Despite the cost, it is critical that you meet with the therapist face-to-face before making your selection. (Programs generally provide for a similar type of interview, usually at no charge.)

After this initial interview, think about these questions: Does the therapist or program counselor seem supportive to you? Do you feel you could disclose to this person your innermost feelings about the assault? Most importantly, what is your gut feeling about the therapist? Qualification are important and, at this point, you should be considering only qualified therapists, but the final decision may be a matter of finding your best emotional match. If you have strong negative feelings toward a particular therapist after an initial interview, it probably isn't a good match, even if the therapist is well qualified. If you are ambivalent, consider meeting with the therapist one more time before making your decision.

Although many psychologists, both men and women, call themselves "feminist" or "nonsexist," you need to decide for yourself if they actually are. Remember that just because a therapist is a woman does not automatically qualify her as nonsexist. Furthermore, today many male therapists are committed to nonsexist treatment and provide excellent counseling. In general, however, it takes considerably more effort for a man to truly understand the impact of sexual assault and sex-role stereotyping on women than it does for a woman.

Evaluating the Course of Therapy and Other Forms of Counseling

Note: The suggestions provided below for evaluating the course of therapy apply to other forms of counseling, such as participating in any form of group therapy or working with a member of the clergy, a spiritual advisor, or others.

Once you've selected a therapist, you can begin your therapy on a trial basis. Make a commitment to work with the therapist for a month, six weeks, or some other limited time period; then reassess your choice. How do you seem to be faring? How effective has the therapist been in addressing the problems you've had due to the assault, including secondary problems such as addiction or depression? Discuss these issues with the therapist. What is his or her assessment of your progress and prognosis for healing?

If the therapist you've selected turns out to have been a poor choice, use the knowledge you've gained to find a better one. The wrong therapist can do more harm than good. However, bear in mind that the course of therapy is not always smooth: backsliding and hostility on your part may all be a part of your healing. Just because you don't feel better every time you leave the office doesn't necessarily mean the therapist isn't helping you.

Stop seeing the therapist if you believe that he or she is actually doing you harm: for example, if the therapist directly or indirectly blames you for the assault; doubts your truthfulness; shows excessive interest in the sexual or violent details of the assault; cannot seem to tolerate your emotional pain or your anger; is unwilling to discuss your concerns about the therapy without becoming hostile toward you or blaming you for your dissatisfaction; is constantly pointing out how the problems you had before the assault contribute greatly to your symptoms; or urges you to continue examining your assault when you can barely make it through the day, for example, when you relapse into addiction, sink into a deep depression, or begin having any of the warning signs listed in the "Cautions" section in the introduction.

You should also be skeptical about a therapist who believes that the negative effects of the assault will go away only if you try harder, forgive the attacker, really want to heal, give up your anger, or have a more positive attitude toward life. You should also be concerned about a therapist who answers "yes," to any of the following questions: Would you ever socialize, flirt, or have sex with a client or someone who used to be your client? Would you ever trade services with a client, for example, accept house repairs in exchange for therapy?

If You Are Referred to a Psychiatrist

If your psychological symptoms are sufficiently severe, a psychiatric evaluation may be suggested. You have nothing to lose by taking a few hours out of your life for a complete psychiatric workup. Be prepared to list your current and past medical problems and medications and your symptoms, their duration and frequency, and any other observations you have made about them.

At the conclusion of the evaluation, medication may or may not be recommended. It is your choice whether to take it or not. You don't have to decide on the spot. It is your right to have the psychiatrist explain your diagnosis and the medication in detail. You may want to look up additional information about your diagnosis and the recommended medication on the Internet or at the library before you make your decision. However, if you have ever attempted or contemplated suicide by overdosing on medication, you *must* obtain medical approval before seeking additional sources of information about a recommended medication.

Medication needs constant monitoring. If you choose to take medication, you may need to contact the psychiatrist several times to change the dosage before the right dosage is established for you. You also will need to call if the negative side effects seem to outweigh the positive effects of the medication. Call the psychiatrist if you feel numb or tired much of the time; cannot concentrate; have physical symptoms such as bleeding, muscle tremors, seizures, dizzy spells, hyperventilation, dark or discolored urine, rashes, inability to urinate, constipation, loss of menstrual period or sex drive, severe headaches, nausea; suicidal thoughts; or have any of the symptoms listed in the "Cautions" section of the introduction.

If your call is not returned promptly, call again. Do not let these side effects go unattended! Finally, be wary of any psychiatrist who does not seem familiar with the medication, who seems to discount your concerns, or who does not return your phone calls regarding your medication. If contacting the psychiatrist is always a problem, consider changing doctors. However, you need to discuss this decision with your therapist or support group first, as well as with the psychiatrist.

Finding a Survivors Group

Many survivors have benefited greatly from participating in a support group. However, being exposed to the emotional pain of other survivors can be overwhelming. If attending a support group results in you developing symptoms such as those listed in the "Cautions" section of the introduction, consult a mental health professional before returning to group.

Some support groups are led by professionals, other by survivors only. Some are identified with a certain faith or denomination. Church-affiliated and survivor-led groups may be free or they may charge very little. Professional-led groups vary in price. Some offer a sliding scale; others do not.

To search for a group appropriate for yourself, consult the resources for finding a therapist or a sexual assault treatment program listed above. Take the same steps to find and a select a survivors group. Later, to assess your progress in group, take the same steps as have been described above for finding, screening, and evaluating an individual therapist or treatment program.

APPENDIX B

Resources

Addictions: Alcohol and Drug Abuse and Eating Disorders

Organizations

If you suffer from an alcohol or drug addition, you will probably need to go to a detox center for medical care as you go through withdrawal. Do not attempt to detox by yourself: withdrawal can lead to medical emergencies. If you suffer from an eating disorder, you may need medical help to stabilize your biochemistry.

Afterward you will need treatment that not only helps you abstain from abusing alcohol, drugs, or food, but also helps you understand why you needed to misuse this substance in the first place. Good treatment teaches you ways to cope with life without an addiction. Your treatment must also help teach you ways to cope with the emotions and situations that you used to manage with alcohol, drugs, or food.

Consider attending an inpatient or outpatient rehabilitation program specific to your addiction or eating disorder. You can obtain the names of treatment centers from the phone book, hospitals, and city or county mental health or social service agencies.

In addition to local programs, there are specialized centers around the country. The names of these programs can be obtained from your doctor or therapist, your local drug or alcohol rehabilitation board or council, a local hospital, or members of twelve-step programs such as Alcoholics Anonymous (AA), Narcotics Anonymous (NA), and Overeaters Anonymous (OA).

All twelve-step programs are free. Information about AA, Al-Anon, Adult Children of Alcoholics, Cocaine Anonymous (CA), NA, Nar-Anon, and OA can be obtained from your telephone directory or local library or by calling the national offices of these organizations.

Books and Other Recommended Materials

Many books, pamphlets, and audio- and videocassettes on issues related to various forms of addiction are available through Hazelden Educational Materials, Box 176, 15251 Pleasant Valley Road, Center City, MN 55012. Call or write for a free catalog.

Alcoholics Anonymous World Services, *The Big Book* and *The Twelve Traditions*. Available from Alcoholics Anonymous World Services, Box 459, Grand Central Station, New York, NY 10163.

Johnson, V. 1973. *I'll Quit Tomorrow*. New York: Harper and Row.

Milam, J., and K. Ketcham. 1982. *Under the Influence: Guide to the Myths and Realities of Alcoholism*. New York: Bantam Books.

Roth, G. 1993. *Feeding the Hungry Heart: The Experience of Compulsive Eating*. New York: Signet.

Sandbeck, T. 1986. *The Deadly Diet: Recovering from Anorexia & Bulimia*. Oakland, CA: New Harbinger Publications, Inc.

Anger-Management

Recommended Books

Matsakis, A. 1996. Chapters 7-9 in *I Can't Get Over It: A Handbook for Trauma Survivors*. Second Edition. Oakland, CA: New Harbinger Publications, Inc.

McKay, M., J. McKay, and P. Rogers. 1989. *When Anger Hurts: Quieting the Storm Within*. Oakland, CA: New Harbinger Publications, Inc.

McKay, M., and P. Rogers. 2000. *The Anger Control Workbook.* Oakland, CA: New Harbinger Publications, Inc.

Potter-Efron, R. 1994. *Angry All the Time: An Emergency Guide to Anger Control.* Oakland, CA: New Harbinger Publications, Inc.

Potter-Efron, R. 2001. *Stop the Anger Now: Workbook for the Prevention, Containment, and Resolution of Anger.* Oakland, CA: New Harbinger Publications, Inc.

Battering: Family Violence

Organizations

You can be directed to sources of help by your local courts, police, library, social service agencies, churches, battered women's shelters, sexual assault centers, community crisis or mental health hotlines, or state chapters of the National Coalition Against Domestic Violence. The National Organization for Victim Assistance in Washington, DC, can direct you to crisis intervention, short-term counseling, medical and legal advice, and referrals for victim-assistance programs across the country. Your local telephone directory or library can provide information on how to contact these organizations.

Crime

Recommended Books

Bard, M., and D. Sangrey. 1986. *The Crime Victim's Book.* Second edition. Secaucus, NJ: Citadel Press. This book explains court procedures, the psychology of crime victims, and ways for victims to claim their rights within government and legal bureaucracies.

NOVA. *Victim Rights and Services: A Legislative Directory.* Available from NOVA, 1730 Park Road, NW, Washington, DC 20010. This publication gives an overview of current federal and state victims' rights and services legislation and victim-compensation programs.

Legal Assistance

Organizations

If you are seeking an attorney with expertise in sexual assault or low-cost or free legal assistance, contact the following: your local courthouse, state bar association, police department, battered women's shelter, sexual assault center, legal aid society, or the law school of a nearby university. Some of these sources may have literature they can send to you or the names of attorneys who volunteer time doing *pro bono* work, that is, legal work for which they do not charge.

In the telephone directory, look in both the white and yellow pages under "Legal Assistance," "Lawyer Referral Services," "Legal Aid," and "Legal Services Plans," for listings. You can also scan the ads in the yellow pages under "Attorneys" or "Lawyers" to look for lawyers who have sliding scale payment plans, offer a half hour of free consultation, or specialize in your problem area. Then call a few of the attorneys you have found. If the lawyer can't help you, he or she may be able to refer you to someone who can. Also, some lawyers work on a contingency basis, which means that if you win your case, they get a percentage of any settlement you receive. If you lose, you don't owe the attorney any money.

Relationships

Recommended Books

Black, J., and G. Enns. 1998. *Better Boundaries: Owning and Treasuring Your Life.* Oakland, CA: New Harbinger Publications, Inc.

Matsakis, A. 1996. *Trust after Trauma: A Guide to Relationships for Trauma Survivors and Those Who Love Them.* Oakland, CA: New Harbinger Publications, Inc.

Paterson, R. 2000. *The Assertiveness Workbook: How to Express Your Ideas and Stand Up for Yourself at Work and in Relationships.* Oakland, CA: New Harbinger Publications, Inc.

Relaxation, Self-Calming, and Self-Care

Recommended Books

Adams, K. 1993. *The Way of the Journal: A Journal Therapy Workbook for Healing.* Second edition. Lutherville, MD: Sidran Press.

Bourne, E. 1995. *The Anxiety and Phobia Workbook.* Second edition. Oakland, CA: New Harbinger Publications, Inc.

Bourne, E. 2001. *Beyond Anxiety and Phobia.* Oakland, CA: New Harbinger Publications, Inc.

Davis, M., M. McKay, and E. Eshelman. 2000. *The Relaxation and Stress Reduction Workbook,* Fifth edition. Oakland, CA: New Harbinger Publications, Inc.

Fanning, P., and H. G. Mitchner. 2001. *The 50 Best Ways to Simplify Your Life.* Oakland, CA: New Harbinger Publications, Inc.

McKay M., K. Beck, and C. Sutker. 2001. *The Self-Nourishment Companion: 52 Inspiring Ways to Take Care of Yourself.* Oakland, CA: New Harbinger Publications, Inc.

McKay, M., P. Fanning, and C. Crowther. 1997. *The Daily Relaxer.* Oakland, CA: New Harbinger Publications, Inc.

Hazelden Educational Materials, Box 176, 15251 Pleasant Valley Road, Center City, MN 55012 carries pamphlets, books, and audiocassette on self-care, relaxation, and a variety of self-calming methods. Call or write for a free catalog.

Sexual Assault

Organizations

Some sexual assault centers offer free or low-cost individual or group therapy; some do not. (See Appendix A.) If your area does not have a sexual assault center, see if there is a battered women's program available. Also check the sources of help listed above under "Crime." You may be able to receive financial help for counseling, medical problems, and other losses incurred as a result of the sexual assault.

Recommended Books

Aranow, V., and M. Lang. 2001. *Journey to Wholeness: Healing from the Trauma of Rape*. Holmes Beach, FL: Learning Publications.

Courtois, C. 1995. *Memory and Abuse: Remembering and Healing the Wounds of Trauma*. Deerfield Beach, FL: Health Communications, Inc.

Bass, E., and L. Davis. 1988. *The Courage to Heal: A Guide for Women Survivors of Child Sexual Abuse*. New York: Perennial (HarperCollins). Also available on audiocassette.

Davis, L. 1990. *The Courage to Heal Workbook: For Women and Men Survivors of Childhood Sexual Abuse*. New York: Harper Collins.

Francisco, P. 1999. *Telling: A Memoir of Rape and Recovery*. New York: Cliff Street Books/Harper Collins.

Lauer, T. 2001. *The Truth about Rape: Emotional, Spiritual, Physical and Sexual Recovery*. Gold River, CA: RapeRecovery.com. This book lists more than 600 associations, Web sites, books, videos, and other resources on a wide range of topics including campus rape, the criminal justice system, sexually transmitted diseases, scar therapy, chronic pain, art therapy, rape-related pregnancy, self-defense, sexuality, and symptoms commonly associated with rape trauma, such as panic disorder, addiction, anger, and guilt.

Scott, K. 1993. *Sexual Assault: Will I Ever Feel Okay Again*? Bloomington, MN: Bethany House.

Trauma Processing and Symptom Management

Recommended Books

Burns, D. 1980. *Feeling Good: The New Mood Therapy*. New York: Signet Books.

Cohen, B., M. Barnes, and A. Rankin. 1995. *Managing Traumatic Stress through Art: Drawing from the Center*. Lutherville, MD: Sidran Press.

Copeland, M. E., and M. Harris. 2000. *Healing the Trauma of Abuse: A Woman's Workbook*. Oakland, CA: New Harbinger Publications, Inc.

Friedberg, F. 2001. *Do-It-Yourself Eye Movement Technique for Emotional Healing*. Oakland, CA: New Harbinger Publications, Inc.

Gallo, F., and H. Vincenzi. 2000. *Energy Tapping: How to Rapidly Eliminate Anxiety, Depression, Cravings, and More Using Energy Psychology*. Oakland, CA: New Harbinger Publications, Inc.

Matsakis, A. 1996. *I Can't Get Over It: A Handbook for Trauma Survivors*. Second edition. Oakland, CA: New Harbinger Publications, Inc.

Paterson, R. 2002. *Your Depression Map: Find the Sources of Your Depression and Chart Your Own Recovery*. Oakland, CA: New Harbinger Publications, Inc.

Rutledge, T. 1997. *The Self-Forgiveness Handbook: A Practical and Empowering Guide*. Oakland, CA: New Harbinger Publications, Inc.

Williams, M. B., and S. Poijula. 2002. *The PTSD Workbook: Simple, Effective Techniques for Overcoming Traumatic Stress Symptoms*. Oakland, CA: New Harbinger Publications, Inc.

References

Allgeier, E. R., and A. R. Allgeier. 1991. *Sexual Interaction*. Lexington, MA: Heath.

Bass, E., and L. Davis. 1988. *The Courage to Heal: A Guide for Women Survivors of Child Sexual Abuse*. New York: Perennial (Harper Collins).

Beck, A. T., and G. Emery. 1985. *Anxiety Disorders and Phobias: A Cognitive Perspective*. New York: Basic Books, Inc.

Becker, J., L. Skinner, G. Abel, and E. Treacy. 1982. Incidence and types of sexual dysfunctions in rape and incest victims. *Journal of Sex & Marital Therapy* 8:65–74.

Cameron, J. 1992. *The Artist's Way: A Spiritual Path to Higher Creativity*. New York: Jeremy P. Tarcher/Putnam, a member of Penguin Putnam, Inc.

Condy, S., D. Templer, R. Brown, and L. Veaco. 1987. Parameters of sexual contact of boys with women. *Archives of Sexual Behavior* 16:5.

Crawford, M., and R. Unger. 2000. *Women and Gender: A Feminist Psychology*. Third edition. Boston: McGraw Hill.

Daniele, Y. 1998. *International Handbook of Multigenerational Legacies of Trauma*. New York: Plenum.

Datcher, M. 2001. *Raising Fences: A Black Man's Love Story*. New York: Harper & Row.

DC Rape Crisis Center, Washington, DC. 2002. E. Dombo, Clinical Director, personal communication Dec. 18, 2002.

Department of Veterans Affairs National Training Program. 1993. *Sexual Trauma: Diagnosis, Treatment, and Related Issues*. Salt Lake City: National Media Development Center.

Duncan, D. 1990. Prevalence of sexual assault victimization among heterosexual and gay/lesbian university students. *Psychological Reports* 55:65–66.

Esterling, B., L. L'Abate, E. Murray, and J. Pennebaker. 1999. Empirical foundations for writing in prevention and psychotherapy: Mental and physical health outcomes. *Clinical Psychology Review* 19:79–96.

FBI Uniform Crime Reports. 1991. *Crime in the United States*. Washington, DC: U.S. Department of Justice.

Forward, S., and C. Buck. 1978. *Betrayal of Innocence: Incest and Its Devastation*. New York, Penguin.

Freeman, A., and F. Zaken-Greenberg. 1989. A cognitive behavioral approach. In *Treating Stress in Families,* edited by C. Figley. New York: Brunner/Mazel.

Gilbert, N. 1993. The wrong response to rape. *Wall Street Journal* June 29, p. A18.

Groth, N., A. Burgess, and L. Holmstron. 1977. Rape: Power, anger, and sexuality. *A Journal of Psychiatry* 134(11):1239–1243.

Hall, C. A., and C. M. Henderson. 1996. Cognitive processing therapy for chronic PTSD from childhood sexual abuse: A case study. *Counseling Psychology Quarterly* 9(4):359.

Hall, R. 1995. *Rape in America: A Reference Handbook*. Santa Barbara, CA: Contemporary World Issues, ABC-CLIO.

Harvey, M. 1996. An Ecological View of Psychological Trauma and Trauma Recovery. *Journal of Traumatic Stress* 9:3–23.

Koss, M., and M. Harvey. 1991. *The Rape Victim: Clinical and Community Interventions.* Newbury Park, CA: Sage Publications.

Krystal, H. 1971. Trauma: consideration of its intensity and chronicity. In *Psychic Traumatization,* edited by. H. Krystal and W. Neiderland. Boston: Little, Brown.

Kubany, E. 1997. Thinking errors, faulty conclusions, and cognitive therapy for trauma-related guilt. *National Center for Post-Traumatic Stress Disorder Quarterly* 7:6–8.

Kubany, E., and F. Manke. 1995. Cognitive therapy for trauma-related guilt: Conceptual bases and treatment outlines. *Cognitive and Behavioral Practice* 2:27–62.

Lauer, T. 2002. *The Truth about Rape: Emotional, Spiritual, Physical, and Sexual Recovery from Rape.* Gold River, CA: www. RapeRecovery.com

Lonsway, K., and L. Fitzgerald. 1994. Rape myths in review. *Psychology of Women Quarterly* 18:133–164.

Media Education Foundation. 1992. *The Date Rape Backlash: The Media and the Denial of Rape.* Northampton, MA: Media Education Foundation. Videocassette.

National Crime Victim Center. 1992. *Rape in America: A Report to the Nation.* Report prepared by the Crime Victims Research and Treatment Center. Charleston, SC: Medical University of South Carolina.

Petrak, J., and B. Hedge. 2002. *The Trauma of Sexual Assault: Treatment, Prevention, and Practice.* West Sussex, England: John Wiley & Sons, Ltd.

Resick, P. A. 1994. Cognitive processing therapy (CPT) for rape-related PTSD and depression. *Clinical Quarterly.* 4(3/4):1, 3–4. Menlo Park, CA: National Center for Post-Traumatic Stress Disorder.

Resick, P. A., and M. K. Schnicke. 1992. Cognitive processing therapy for sexual assault victims. *Journal of Consulting and Clinical Psychology* 60(5):748–756.

Robinson, T. 2000. Making the hurt go away: Psychological and spiritual healing for African-American women survivors of childhood incest. *Journal of Multicultural Counseling & Development* 28(3):160–176.

Roiphe, K. 1993. *The Morning After: Sex, Fear, and Feminism on Campus*. Boston: Little, Brown.

Russell, D. 1975. The *Politics of Rape: The Victim's Perspective*. New York: Stein and Day Publishers.

Shay, J. 2002. *Odysseus in America: Combat Trauma and the Trials of Homecoming*. New York: Scribner.

Shephard, B. 2001. *A War of Nerves: Soldiers and Psychiatrists in the Twentieth Century*. Cambridge, MA: Harvard University Press.

Terr, L. C. 1983. Time sense following psychic trauma: A clinical study of ten adults and twenty children. *American Journal of Orthopsychiatry* 53:244–261.

Ullman, S., and H. H. Filipas. 2001. Predictors of PTSD symptom severity and social reactions in sexual assault victims. *Journal of Traumatic Stress* 14(2):369–389.

van Berlo, W., and B. Ensink, 2000. Problems with sexuality after sexual assault. *Annual Review of Sex Research* 2:235–236.

van der Kolk, B., A. McFarlane, and L. Weisaeth, eds. 1996. *Traumatic Stress: The Effects of Overwhelming Stress on Mind, Body, and Society*. New York: Guilford Press.

Wade, C., and S. Cirese. 1991. *Human Sexuality*. San Diego: Harcourt, Brace, Jovanovich.

Washington Post. 15 March, 1991. "Reported Sexual Assaults Increase Sharply in Area."

Winston, S. 2001. *What Every Trauma Therapist Should Know about Panic, Phobia, and OCD*. Audiotape 01ISTSS-71 ISTSS (International Society for Traumatic Stress Studies) 17th Annual Meeting, Fairmont Hotel, New Orleans, LA, December, 2001.

Wolf, N. 1991. *The Beauty Myth*. New York: William Morrow.

Some Other
New Harbinger Titles

Eating Mindfully, Item 3503 $13.95

Sex Talk, Item 2868 $12.95

Everyday Adventures for the Soul, Item 2981 $11.95

A Woman's Addiction Workbook, Item 2973 $18.95

The Daughter-In-Law's Survival Guide, Item 2817 $12.95

PMDD, Item 2833 $13.95

The Vulvodynia Survival Guide, Item 2914 $15.95

Love Tune-Ups, Item 2744 $10.95

The Deepest Blue, Item 2531 $13.95

The 50 Best Ways to Simplify Your Life, Item 2558 $11.95

Brave New You, Item 2590 $13.95

Loving Your Teenage Daughter, Item 2620 $14.95

The Hidden Feelings of Motherhood, Item 2485 $14.95

The Woman's Book of Sleep, Item 2418 $14.95

Pregnancy Stories, Item 2361 $14.95

The Women's Guide to Total Self-Esteem, Item 2418 $13.95

Thinking Pregnant, Item 2302 $13.95

The Conscious Bride, Item 2132 $12.95

Juicy Tomatoes, Item 2175 $13.95

Facing 30, Item 1500 $12.95

The Money Mystique, Item 2221 $13.95

High on Stress, Item 1101 $13.95

Perimenopause, 2nd edition, Item 2345 $16.95

The Infertility Survival Guide, Item 2477 $16.95

Call **toll free, 1-800-748-6273,** or log on to our online bookstore at **www.newharbinger.com** to order. Have your Visa or Mastercard number ready. Or send a check for the titles you want to New Harbinger Publications, Inc., 5674 Shattuck Ave., Oakland, CA 94609. Include $4.50 for the first book and 75¢ for each additional book, to cover shipping and handling. (California residents please include appropriate sales tax.) Allow two to five weeks for delivery.

Prices subject to change without notice.